20 Minutes to Dinner

Quick, Low-Fat, Low-Calorie Vegetarian Meals

by Bryanna Clark Grogan

Book Publishing Company
Summertown, Tennessee

Cover photo: David Hawkins
Author photo: Brian Grogan
Cover design: Bev Lacy, State of the Art
Interior design: Cynthia Holzapfel
Illustrations: Otis Maly

Pictured on the cover: Grilled Vegetable Salad (p. 86), Pasta Primavera Salad (p. 83)

Printed in the United States by   The Book Publishing Company
                                   P.O. Box 99
                                   Summertown, TN 38483
                                   800-695-2241

01 00 99 98 97   1 2 3 4 5 6

ISBN 1-57067-027-7

Grogan, Bryanna Clark
     20 minutes to dinner : quick, low-fat, low calorie, vegetarian
  meals / by Bryanna Clark Grogan.
        p.   cm.
     Includes Index.
     ISBN 1-57067-027-7 (alk. paper)
     1. Vegetarian cookery. 2. Quick and easy cookery. 3. Low-fat
  diet--Recipes.   I. Title.
TX837.G675 1997
641.5'636--dc21   9640101
                                             CIP

Calculations for the nutritional analyses in this book are based on the average number of servings listed with the recipes and the average amount of an ingredient, if a range is called for. Calculations are rounded up to the nearest gram. If two options for an ingredient are listed, the first one is used. Not included are optional ingredients, serving suggestions, or fat used for frying, unless the amount of fat is specified in the recipe.

table of contents

DEDICATION
This one's for my wonderful, talented, and busy daughters, Bethany, Sarah, and Justine, and also for Sylvie, a daughter of the heart.

ACKNOWLEDGMENTS
Many thanks to Dr. Andrew Weil for his advice and comments. Also to my mom, Eve Urbina, and my husband Brian, for their constant love and support. Thanks also to my editors, Michael Cook and Cynthia Holzapfel, and all the BPC folks, for their faith in me and their cheerfulness.

introduction

It's ironic that, in this age of time-saving devices, fast cars, rapid transit, and the "information highway," we seem to have so little time to devote to one of the most important areas of our lives—food. For many years, I rebelled against this trend and refused to cater to it, but, alas, I often find myself caught up in the "not-enough-time" bind! I also have grown-up children who work full-time or have small children, and don't have my interest in food. They just want something fast, nutritious, and delicious that doesn't cost the earth! So those are the criteria for the recipes in this book.

There are quite a few "quick-cook" books on the market, many of them low-fat, and several vegetarian ones, but I believe that this is one of the very few that presents delicious, egg- and dairy-free, vegetarian, ultra-low-fat, AND quick-cooking recipes.

I purposely did not format this book along the lines of "follow-this-menu-and-recipe/shopping-plan," because most of us don't have time to go shopping every night for specific recipes. If you follow the shopping advice in Chapter I, you'll be able to make spur of the moment meals from your "pantry."

I've furnished you with a lot of solid cooking information and recipes that are also guides. This way you can tailor meals and recipes to your liking and to what is available to you, giving as many reasonable substitution possibilities as I can, a number of which can be helpful if you have allergies to specific foods. I want this to be the sort of book you reach for for ideas, when you're in a jam, not just for specific recipes. Most of the recipes in this book can be made in about 20 minutes, from start to finish. Some go over a bit; many are even faster than that. I've avoided recipes that call for excessive stirring, fussing, or watching, since I know that when you are rushed you are often trying to cook a couple of things at the same time. A blender and a food processor are necessary for many recipes (a "given" really, for chopping quickly), but such devices as microwave ovens or pressure cookers are optional (directions will be given where applicable). I decided not to include slow-cooker recipes, even though they are convenient and timesaving, partly as a way to weed out recipes and partly because "timesaving" does not necessarily translate to "fast." It goes without saying that I think the recipes in this book are delicious and are ones that I use regularly, but I want to assure you that I've also tried to keep the cost per serving of these recipes as low as possible by not using too many ready-to-eat or convenience products. Chapter II includes a number of quick-to-make homemade alternatives to store-bought basics if you are cost-conscious or want more control over the ingredients in your food.

I hope that these recipes will help to streamline your busy-day meals and give you more time and energy for your family, for relaxation and quiet time (which is as necessary to health as good food), and for those activities which enrich your soul.

nutrition, cooking & shopping tips

a low-fat vegetarian diet: your gateway to better health

A vegetarian eating plan which gets about 10% of its calories from fat (espoused by such experts as Dr. Dean Ornish, Dr. Neal Barnard, and Dr. John McDougall) makes a lot of sense for many people in our society. It can help you lose weight and keep it off without feeling deprived, because you can eat to satisfaction when you are consuming mostly complex carbohydrates like vegetables, fruits, grains, and legumes. It can also reverse heart disease without drugs and surgery and can prevent cancer and other degenerative diseases. It has proven to be an immune-system-supporting diet, and a great many people (myself included) generally feel healthier and more energetic when eating a low-fat, plant-based diet. It is also a powerful way to contribute to the sustainable future of our planet and to a way of life that "does no harm."

But what about these "new" high-protein weight-loss diets that are all the rage right now? For one thing, there isn't anything new about this idea (except that some of the fat recommended is monosaturated). This diet was all the rage in the 70s too. And it didn't last for the simple reason that it wasn't healthful and it didn't make you feel very good. I went on it myself for about a week and dragged around like a zombie with no energy until I came to my senses!

A lot of the hoop-la stems from claims that our bodies quickly store low-fat, high-carbohydrate foods as fat, especially if you are insulin-resistant. Medical experts point out, however, that insulin-resistant individuals are no more likely to gain weight on a low-fat diet than insulin-sensitive people, no matter what the source of calories.

The facts remain—there is no quick-fix diet, and losing weight is not the only concern in a healthful lifestyle. Getting too much protein is still a problem for your kidneys, which may be over-stressed by filtering the waste products from excess protein in the body. The more protein you eat, the harder the kidneys have to work, which may result in impaired kidney function.

And dribbling pools of olive oil on your food will still result in the ingestion of far too many calories for the type of lifestyle most of us lead. We aren't Greek peasants hoeing the fields all day or carrying heavy loads on long treks! They are expending huge levels of calories just making a living! AND the Greeks, who have been the subjects of many dietary studies, eat far MORE bread and vegetables (and LESS meat and saturated fat) than the average North American, something that is not taken into consideration in these new fad diets. Neither is the WAY they eat, consuming the biggest meal of the day at noon, in a leisurely manner, surrounded by family.

The healthiest, longest-living, most disease-free people eat high-carbohydrate, low-protein diets. Fat levels vary, but cultures which eat very little fat and animal protein seem to have lower levels of various types of cancer.

Fads come and go, but wisdom remains—the best diet FOR HEALTH as well as weight-control, according to what we know to date, is one that is high in complex carbohydrates (whole grains, beans, fruits, vegetables), relatively low in protein and fat, and moderate in calories.

Most of the recipes in this book limit the fat to about 10 to 20 percent of the total calories, but a few go a little over (some have options that add a little more fat). These can be balanced with lower-fat recipes, or you may not worry about keeping your fat intake that low. Certainly, eating under 20% of calories from fat in your diet will give you a head start on most North Americans! We give calorie counts for our recipes too, because some people have an easier time controlling their weight if they pay attention to calories as well as fat grams. This should not be done slavishly, and calories should never go below about 1,200 a day—moderation and portion control is the key. Remember that overeating pasta or fat-free cookies, or forgetting that a bakery bagel can outweigh five slices of bread, can lead to weight gain. Eat those vegetables!

At first glance, the low-fat vegetarian way of eating sounds restrictive: no animal products, including eggs and dairy products; no REGULAR consumption of olives, avocados, nuts, and seeds; and virtually no oil or margarine used in cooking. However, I have found it to be very liberating. As Dr. Dean Ornish says, it's often easier to make big changes in your life than little ones, and big changes certainly make more of an impact. The conservative 30%-of-calories-from-fat recommended by the American Heart Association will not result in weight loss or reversal of heart disease.

When you cook with virtually no added fats, there's no worrying about measuring and draining, counting fat grams, or stressing out over trans-fatty acids. You don't have to decide whether or not to buy refined, unrefined, expeller-pressed, or cold-pressed oils, or

debate the merits of butter vs. margarine. Most of the fat you ingest will be in its unrefined, unextracted form as part of the grains and soybean products you eat. Otherwise, you might use a tiny amount of flavorful extra-virgin olive oil or neutral canola oil (both monosaturated), Chinese roasted sesame oil, or a high-quality, dairy-free margarine. When you aren't eating meat, fish, and poultry, you don't have to weigh portions, cut off fat, and discard skin. You don't have to read the labels of dairy products for fat content or throw egg yolks down the drain.

You DO have before you a vast array of foods to choose from, many that you perhaps weren't familiar with before—soy products and seitan from the Far East; exotic vegetables like broccoli rabe and portobello mushrooms; grain dishes like polenta, bulgur wheat, and couscous; dried legumes such as anasazi beans and red lentils; and herbs and spices from all over the world. Added to such "old familiars" as potatoes, pasta, breads, common vegetables, dried peas and beans, and fruits (and a few "health food" basics such as nutritional yeast), you can actually have a much more interesting and varied diet than you had before.

Most of these recipes are based on what might be called the "Mediterranean/Asian model," using lots of grains, fruits, and vegetables in the style of one of the many varied and flavorful cuisines of those parts of the world. Sometimes I borrow from one and add to the other—for instance, using Asian tofu instead of ricotta cheese in an Italian dish. This "vegan Italian lean cuisine" makes a lot of sense in the light of new studies that urge men to introduce more soy and tomatoes into a low-fat, high-fiber, high-complex-carbohydrate diet for prevention of prostrate cancer!

You'll learn about flavoring foods in a new way too, breaking your dependence on fats, cream, and smoked meats for flavoring (which often smothers the natural flavors of fresh, seasonal, high-quality foods). We replace these with ingredients like wine, natural flavoring extracts, citrus zest, garlic, onions, herbs and spices, broth, juices, soy sauce, tomatoes, chiles, vegetable purees, roasted vegetables, dried mushrooms, maple syrup, . . . the list goes on. We can use marinades and roasting techniques (quick versions, of course!). Think flavor, not fat!

World-renowned chefs like Jacques Pépin, Jean-Marc Fullsack, and Joyce Goldstein are replacing the fats in their recipes with new flavor secrets too, so you are in good company!

how much fat is too much?

What I do not want to contribute to with this book is a paranoia about fats or encourage a new eating disorder. I view this eating style as liberation, not deprivation. I shake my head when I hear stories about people who won't even have a bite of a salad with a few olives chopped up in it at a potluck, or those who refuse to eat tofu, one of our most versatile and valuable vegetarian foods, because they think of it as a "high-fat" food (more about this on p. 10). These people need to "lighten up" on their attitudes, rather than their diets!

Unless you have a very severe medical problem which demands strict adherence to the 10%-of-calories-from-fat principle, you can relax a bit when you go out to dinner at a restaurant or at a friend's. I politely refuse non-vegetarian foods, but I eat moderately of nuts, seeds, avocado, olives, oil, and even deep-fried foods or dishes made with coconut milk when I go out (which is infrequent)—without guilt and with great enjoyment. I know I can't eat like this all the time (nor do I want to, because my body doesn't take kindly to it any-more!), but I believe it is my style of day-to-day eating that makes the difference.

The reason that my previous books have been designated "ALMOST no-fat," or "low-fat," is that we must have a little fat in our diets, in the form of essential fatty acids, in order to absorb fat-soluble nutrients (vitamins A, D, E, and K) and keep our skin, hair, and nails shiny and healthy. Omega-3 fatty acids and omega-6 fatty acids act as anti-inflammatory agents, may protect against heart attacks by thinning the blood, and may help the immune system.

Many people take flaxseed oil, evening primrose oil, and other oils for their essential fatty acid content. However, Dr. Andrew Weil,

author of *Natural Health, Natural Medicine,* and Udo Erasmus, author of *Fats That Heal, Fats That Kill,* agree that healthy people who eat a diet rich in whole grains, legumes, and leafy green vegetables don't need to take these oils therapeutically. Dr. Weil recommends those of us on an almost-no-fat eating plan eat 1 tablespoon of freshly ground flaxseed a day (this is the equivalent of about 1 teaspoon of oil, but with fiber and other nutrients intact). This can be sprinkled on cereal or other foods.* Flaxseed is the richest vegetarian source of omega-3s and can balance a diet that includes reasonable amounts of soy products, a rich source of omega-6s.

Other vegetarian foods that contain essential fatty acids, besides high-fat nuts, seeds, and oils, are: leafy green vegetables and herbs, especially purslane and borage; whole grains and grain sprouts; wheat germ; sesame seeds (ground); legumes and legume sprouts; fruit seeds (such as in berries, figs, and papayas); and sprouted seeds. Of these foods, only the wheat germ and sesame seeds are high-fat foods, and these can be used in small amounts.

You're apt to see the quantity of fat in a food measured as a percentage of calories in that food. This is because nutritionists are recommending what proportion of calories in our diet should come from fat. Standard recommendations for good health are currently 30% of calories from fat. Recent reports from researchers recommend much lower levels—around 10% to 15%—to achieve weight loss and protect against heart disease and cancer.

After eating a low-fat diet for a while, you

---

*Seeds can be freshly ground each day in an inexpensive electric spice/coffee grinder. Freeze any leftovers. Drink plenty of water when you eat ground flaxseed.

probably won't need to count fat grams at all, but in the beginning, it might help you to see how much fat you are eating (or how little). A moderately active man weighing about 150 lbs. can eat about 25 grams of fat a day to stay in the 10%-calories-from-fat range; a moderately active woman weighing 130 lbs. can eat 20 grams daily. If you are less active, eat a couple of grams less; if you are more active, you can eat a few more. If your ideal weight is more or less than this, adjust your fat intake accordingly.

It's not too difficult to calculate the percentage of calories from fat that you eat each day. A gram of fat will provide 9 calories when consumed. If over a day's time you've eaten 20 grams of fat and 1,800 calories, you can calculate the percentage of calories from fat like this:

This is a fairly easy example to calculate.

> 20 grams fat x 9 calories per gram =
> 180 calories from fat
> 180 calories from fat/1,800 total calories =
> 10% of calories from fat

When the numbers get more complicated (72 grams of fat and 2,330 calories, for example), round up a little and get a close approximation (multiply fat grams by 10 instead of 9, so that 72 grams x 10 = 720 calories; 720 calories is a little less than ⅓ of 2,330, so the percentage is around 30%).

Although considering the percentage of fat in your total diet can be useful, looking at individual foods or recipes this way can be misleading. A food can be low in fat, but be so low in calories as well that the percentage of fat to calories can look deceivingly high (as with regular tofu, which has only 82 calories in a 4 oz. serving, but half those calories come from fat).

A calorie-dense food, such as one high in sugar, might have a lower percentage of calories from fat, but actually contain more fat per serving. If you planned on eating quite a bit of just one food, you might want to look at the percentage of calories from fat in that one food, but we rarely eat like this. The best way to keep your fat level down to about 10% of total calories is to not use added oils and fats, eat only plant foods, and keep high-fat plant foods to a bare minimum.

Tofu: A High-Fat Food?

Tofu deserves some additional mention because so much has been written about its high percentage of fat. As I demonstrated in the previous paragraph, 50% of the calories in regular tofu come from fat. But the total amount of calories in tofu are very low, much lower than equivalent amounts of avocado, nuts, etc., and much lower than eggs, oil, and solid cooking fats. When I use 1 lb. of regular tofu in my basic recipe for 18 cupcakes, each cupcake has about 1 gram of fat (and reduced-fat tofu lowers it even more). A traditional, "low-fat" recipe for 12 cupcakes or muffins made with 1 large egg and ¼ cup of oil (not counting any nuts that might be added) would contain about 58 grams of fat or close to 5 grams per cupcake or muffin.

The truth is that soyfoods are good for us. Study after study confirms that soyfoods of all kinds can significantly lower blood cholesterol, are an excellent source of iron in the diet, and may have a major role in cancer prevention.

Tofu is probably the most versatile soyfood since it can be used not only as a meat substitute, but also as a replacement for high-fat dairy products and eggs. Also, tofu and soymilk provide a natural way to ingest essential omega-6 fatty acids. As long as fruits, vegetables, whole grains, and legumes make up the majority of your diet (and nuts, oils, seeds, olives, and avocados are only occasional treats), tofu, soymilk, and other soyfoods can play important supporting roles.

If you are still concerned about the fat in tofu and soyfoods, investigate the lower-fat soy products that are coming into the market: reduced-fat soymilk, regular tofu, and silken tofu. I have used reduced-fat tofu throughout the book to demonstrate how you can use it to cut back on fat even more than with full-fat tofu.

If you cannot find reduced-fat soy products in your area, you may substitute the full-fat products without affecting the outcome of the recipes, but the fat content will increase slightly.

There are many low-fat vegetarian hot dogs and burgers on the market too, and textured vegetable protein is naturally almost fat-free (see p. 26).

Dietary Fat for Children and Teenagers

Please note that although for many adults a very low-fat, fairly low-protein, high-fiber diet may be the best choice, children and teenagers need a higher-fat, higher-protein, and lower-fiber diet. They can eat the same foods that you do, but let them eat often, and add higher-fat foods (nut and seed butters, avocados) and high-protein foods (nuts, seeds, tofu, soymilk, and other soy products, beans, nutritional yeast, wheat germ) to make their diets at least 20% of calories from fat. Avoid excessive consumption of juice, soft drinks, and coffee.

Steam-Frying

Steam-frying is a method I use in many of my recipes to reduce the fat content but retain flavor. It simply means sautéing or stir-frying without fat. To do this, use a heavy skillet or well-seasoned wok, either nonstick or lightly oiled with about ½ tsp. of oil brushed on with your fingertips.

Heat your pan over high heat, and add your chopped onions or other vegetables and 1 or 2 tablespoons of liquid (water, broth, or wine), depending on the amount of vegetables. Cook over high heat until the liquid starts to evaporate, stirring with a spatula or wooden spoon. Keep doing this until the vegetables are done to your liking; add just enough liquid to keep the vegetables from sticking to the bottom of the pan—you don't want to stew them!

You can brown onions perfectly by this method. As soon as the natural sugar in the onions starts to brown on the bottom and edges of the pan, add a little liquid and scrape the browned onions, mixing them into the liquids and around into the other cooking onions. Keep doing this until the onions are soft and brown, being careful not to scorch them.

a word about nutrition

A full discussion of nutrition is beyond the scope of this book. I urge you to consult the books now available on the subject so you will have solid nutritional information to work with.

Here are a few things to keep in mind:

Anyone who eats a varied diet and enough calories to maintain their body weight and energy level is getting enough protein (perhaps more than enough).*

As long as you eat a variety of foods, you don't need to worry about combining proteins (eating beans and grains at the same meal, etc.)

All known nutrients (with the possible exceptions of vitamin B_{12} and vitamin D) are adequately supplied by a varied diet of any whole, vegetarian foods which supply you with enough calories for good health. You can meet your requirement for vitamin B_{12} by taking 25 micrograms each week in pill form, or eating nutritional yeast flakes that have B_{12} added. If you expose your face and arms to the sun (even when it's cloudy) for 10 to 15 minutes a day, your body will naturally produce enough vitamin D. This amount of exposure will be sufficient if you live in the southern areas of the U.S. I recommend that you take some vitamin D from a vegetable source during the winter if you live in a northern climate or are nursing or pregnant.

Over-consumption of protein and salt, not under-consumption of calcium, may be the most important factors contributing to osteoporosis. World health statistics show that the disease is most common in countries where dairy products are consumed in large quantities. Good vegetarian sources of calcium are kale, dried legumes, sesame meal, blackstrap molasses, leafy green vegetables, carob, soy flour, tofu made with calcium salts (most commercial tofu is these days), dried fruit, nutritional yeast, corn tortillas and masa harina, acorn squash, and sea vegetables. If you are still concerned about calcium, take calcium carbonate, the cheapest, most concentrated, and easily absorbed form. Get plenty of exercise, avoid alcohol and tobacco, and reduce your consumption of caffeine and soft drinks.

You do not need to eat red meat for iron. Some excellent vegetarian sources of iron are sea vegetables, prunes and other dried fruits, prune juice, nutritional yeast, blackstrap molasses, beans, soyfoods, whole grains, potatoes, sesame meal, and fresh peas. Dairy products lack iron and can block iron absorption. Your iron absorption is increased by eating plenty of foods rich in vitamin C, such as fruits and vegetables, not drinking caffeinated beverages (including tea) with meals, and cooking in cast iron pots. The Chinese have excellent iron levels despite high levels of fiber and low levels of red meat in their diet.

If you are pregnant, nursing, ill, or under stress, you will need to include more concentrated proteins (tofu, tempeh, textured vegetable protein, other soyfoods, and seitan). If you are expending large amounts of energy, you will need more grains, fruits, and high-carbohydrate vegetables.

Eat a variety of whole foods in as close to their natural state as possible.

---

*See *Diet for a Small Planet* by Frances Moore Lappé (New York: Ballantine Books, 1991)

ingredient substitutions
for allergies and special diets

Soyfoods: Most of the recipes in this book call for "reduced-fat" (sometimes called "lite") soymilk and tofu of various kinds (see p. 185 for more details on different types of tofu). If you cannot find the "reduced-fat" variety in your area, you can use the ordinary varieties without affecting the outcome. The fat content per serving will be slightly higher.

To make inexpensive, homemade, "reduced-fat" soymilk, simply dilute 1 quart (1 L) of regular commercial full-fat soymilk with 1 quart (1 L) of water. Full-fat soymilk is so rich that this diluted version still tastes good. It has half the fat, and it costs about the same as dairy milk! If it is not sweet enough for you, try adding 1 tablespoon of maple syrup per quart of diluted soymilk.

To fortify non-dairy milks with calcium, add 1½ tablespoons calcium carbonate powder to the diluted 2 quarts (2 L) of soymilk (or add ¾ tablespoon to 1 quart or liter of other non-dairy milk). Shake well before pouring. This will provide between 300 and 325 mg calcium per cup—about the same as dairy milk.

If you are allergic to soy products, you can substitute rice, almond, or potato-based "milks" and "milk" powders for the soymilk called for, but be aware that only soymilk curdles like dairy milk when an acid, like lemon juice, is added, so it's difficult to make a thick buttermilk substitute with anything but soymilk. Soy also acts as a "dough conditioner," similar to eggs, when used in yeast breads and baking.

Tofu is difficult to replace in creamy mixtures, but not impossible. In blended mixtures such as sauces, dressings, puddings, pie fillings, shakes, soups, spreads, dips, cheese substitutes, etc., you can experiment with replacing the tofu called for with an equal amount of cooked rice, millet, barley, oatmeal, cornmeal mush, mashed potato, or white beans. If you don't mind a few extra fat grams, a small amount of raw cashews added to one of these no-fat, starchy ingredients can add flavor and creaminess (1 ounce of raw cashews, or about 4 tablespoons, contains about 12 grams of fat, but a little can go a long way).

As meat substitutes, tofu, textured vegetable protein, and tempeh can be replaced by seitan, a wheat gluten product (p. 182), canned Chinese gluten products (check for soy sauce in seitan and gluten products), firm mushrooms, chick-peas, or other beans. There is a chick-pea miso made by Miso Master in Rutherford, North Carolina, available in some health food stores.

For soy-free alternatives to various Chinese sauces, like brown bean, hoisin, black bean, and Szechuan chile bean paste, see p. 182.

For soy sauce or tamari (or liquid aminos), you can use this quite tasty mixture:

Soy-Free Soy Sauce or Tamari Replacement
Mix ¾ c. water, broth, or mushroom soaking liquid with 1 T. EACH yeast extract (like Marmite), soy-free gravy browner (like Kitchen Bouquet), and salt.

This replaces 15 T. (slightly less than 1 c.) of soy sauce. If you have a soy allergy, substitute this mixture tablespoon for tablespoon for the soy sauce called for in the recipes in this book.

To replace some of the complex qualities that a good fermented soy sauce or tamari supplies, try adding wine, broth, and/or mushroom broth or concentrate to the dish, in addition to the soy sauce substitute above.

Check labels for soy protein in broth powders and bouillon cubes and other packaged products.

In this book, I have tried to indicate alternates to soy wherever possible, without adding excessive fat or compromising the taste. I have provided recipes for soy-free, low-fat mayonnaise (p. 32), "sour cream" (p. 33), a cream cheese substitute (p. 36), cheesy sauces (p. 43), and creamy pasta sauce (p. 71), as well as many soups, dips, and dressings (check the Index under "soy-free"). See also *The Uncheese Cookbook* by Joanne Stepaniak, which has many soy-free recipes.

NOTE: Recipes will be marked "Can Be Soy-Free" if there are substitutions for the soyfood ingredients listed in the recipe. Recipes with no soy products are marked "Soy Free."

Salt: Salt can be reduced to your taste, replaced with salt substitutes, or, in some cases, herbal blends. But be aware that processed foods and cheese account for over 75% of the salt in the American diet. You may not need to reduce salt when eating unprocessed, dairy-free foods. (Soyfoods, such as tofu, are naturally very low in sodium, but milk products are naturally high in sodium.) You may wish to use a low-sodium (sometimes called "lite") soy sauce. Cooking experts know that salt used in cooking enhances and balances flavors, smooths out bitterness, and increases sweetness. It also affects the way food smells. Dr. Michael Klaper, in his book *Vegan Nutrition, Pure and Simple*, notes, "The favorable balance between potassium to sodium [in the vegan diet] is especially healthful...and is probably the main factor in the delightful low-to-normal blood pressure seen in so many vegans."

Sweeteners: The use of sugar is always controversial. My take on it is that we get too complaisant when we eat "natural" sugars, such as concentrated grain or fruit sugars. Researchers have found that ingesting sugar in the form of sucrose, glucose, fructose, honey, or orange juice all led to a significant drop in white blood cells, reducing the effectiveness of the immune system.

So, I leave it up to you. I eat desserts once a week at most, and I use Sucanat (granulated sugar cane juice) and turbinado sugar, an unbleached sugar. Use ordinary white and brown sugar if you like (cane sugars are bleached with bone ash, but beet sugar is not), or you can use granulated Fruitsource, a concentrated grain and fruit sweetener, if you prefer (this isn't as sweet as sugar). Molasses (a good source of calcium and iron) lends special flavor to some desserts. You can substitute liquid Fruitsource, maple syrup, concentrated fruit syrup, or grain syrups for honey and molasses; just be aware that they are generally half as sweet as honey and far more costly.

Frozen fruit juice concentrates are inexpensive sweeteners for fruit desserts and some baking, and will replace some of the liquid in the recipe, as well. The recipe must have a fair amount of liquid to start with. For each ½ cup sugar and 1½ cups liquid, substitute 1½ cups of frozen apple juice (a 12-oz. can) or other sweet juice concentrate, adding 1 tsp. of baking soda to counteract the acid in the juice. To use less liquid, boil it down by half.

Alcohol: Alcoholic beverages, such as wine, beer, and liqueurs can add rich flavor to no-fat cooking. Most of the alcohol evaporates during cooking, but, if you prefer, you can use a good-quality, non-alcoholic wine or beer, or in some cases, juice. Dry sherry can be replaced by a mixture of frozen apple juice concentrate and non-alcoholic dry white wine, or a fairly sweet, non-alcoholic wine. Apple, cranberry, or unsweetened white grape juice, or just plain water with a tablespoon or two of balsamic vinegar are other options. Liqueurs and hard liquor, such as brandy, rum, and whiskey, can often be replaced by an appropriate flavor extract, but use less extract than you would liqueur.

Caffeine: Coffee contains caffeine, a highly-addictive substance that can affect insulin balance, so I recommend the use of Swiss water-decaffeinated organic coffee or a good coffee substitute. (I also use good-quality, water-decaffeinated tea.)

Corn: If you are allergic to corn (more common than you may think), you can substitute wheat starch for cornstarch—it can be used exactly like cornstarch. The other starch I like to use is potato, but it should not be boiled like corn or wheat starch—it only needs to get hot to thicken. I find tapioca starch and arrowroot rather slimy in some preparations, but you can experiment.

Semolina cereal can replace cornmeal in polenta, cereals, and baking. Millet makes a good cornmeal mush substitute in blended mixtures. You can use wheat tortillas, and there are several types of baked, no-fat chips on the market now which contain no corn.

Wheat: Those who are allergic to wheat can find many new wheat-free products in natural food stores—too numerous to mention. Wheat tortillas can be replaced by corn, and we are fortunate to have widely-available, Italian-style rice pastas now, in the form of macaroni, spirals, spaghetti, fettuccine, and lasagne noodles. You can also buy a type of "couscous" called Riz Cous (Lunenberg Farms), made from rice.

The meat substitute seitan, or mun chai'ya, the canned Chinese vegetarian "roast duck" (both made from wheat gluten) can be replaced with tofu, tempeh, or textured vegetable protein, or commercial products made from them.

Yeasted Products: If you think you might have a problem with yeast allergies, you can substitute a type of unfermented soy sauce called "liquid aminos" for regular soy sauce and perhaps yeast extract or dark or red miso. It doesn't have the rich flavor of fermented soy sauce, and it is far more expensive, but is a real boon for those that must avoid fermented foods. Check for it in your local health food store. I can think of no practical substitutes for light miso or certain fermented Chinese products like doufu-ru (Chinese fermented bean curd, which has a strong "blue cheese" type of flavor). Nutritional yeast is acceptable for people on a yeast-free diet; it is an inactive yeast.

Seventh Day Adventist vegan cookbooks have good ideas for people who can't eat soy or fermented foods, and for using grains in unusual ways—check the entry for ABC Vegetarian Foods under Mail Order Sources (p. 186). They have an 800 number and supply many strict vegetarian cookbooks that use no extracted oils, strong spices, sugar, alcohol, fermented products, or chemical leavenings; they do use baking yeast and nuts.

Please keep these ideas in mind as you read through the recipes—I have tried to supply alternatives within appropriate recipes, but, because of space, this wasn't always practical.

organic ingredients

Should you only buy organically grown foods? That depends on several things: how important it is for you to support organic farming; the amount of pesticide residues in specific foods; the availability of organic foods in your area; and your budget. Organic foods are usually more expensive, but prices are improving. You will likely be spending less money if you eliminate animal products from your diet, so you will probably be able to afford better-quality organic foods (many supermarket produce sections have organic foods now). Organic dry foods bought in bulk, such as beans and grains, are usually quite reasonable.

If money is the chief concern, consider buying at least some organic foods (peanuts and raisins should always be organic, since they contain the highest amounts of pesticide residues of any vegetable products). Grow whatever you can, even in pots (herbs, sprouts, lettuce, greens, etc.). Fresh, local organic produce is at its cheapest in season and even cheaper if you buy it directly from the producer. Many organic farmers now offer Community Supported Agriculture (CSA) programs—you pay a flat fee per month or week (or buy an annual "share" in the farm), and they deliver an assortment of seasonal produce to your door for several months of the year. This is a great boon to city dwellers and organic farmers alike.

More and more organic frozen, canned, and packaged products are available these days, including such quick-cooking essentials as canned diced tomatoes, tomato sauce and paste, and spaghetti sauce.

Even if you can't always buy organic, try to buy the freshest, highest-quality food you can afford. The success of quick, low-fat cooking depends on your use of good quality ingredients. For the most part, buy seasonally and locally grown produce if you can.

tips for quick, low-fat cooking

Shopping

If you live in a large city, you should have no trouble purchasing everything called for in this book. Most large supermarkets on both coasts have such items as tofu, Chinese black bean sauce, and basmati rice. Natural food stores carry many exotic items and, in larger centers, there will be ethnic markets to fill in the gaps. If you live in a rural area, or a Midwestern town where tofu is still virtually unknown, you may have to use more of the recipes from the Basics chapter, and mail order some foods (see p. 186), but you may be able to find a food co-op or persuade your supermarket manager to order you cases of shelf-stable items such as silken tofu, soymilk, etc. Whenever possible, I have suggested substitutions for exotic items.

Keep a running shopping list so that you don't run out of crucial items. Or use a "Master Shopping List" of all the items you normally buy (perhaps on your computer), so that you can just check off items you need, and you'll be reminded of things you might have forgotten. Keep "emergency provisions" for full meals on hand, in case you can't get to the store—ingredients for tacos, for instance (frozen tortillas, bottled salsa, canned, no-fat vegetarian beans, cabbage, and onions). Shop once a week AT MOST, unless you live very near your favorite stores, and always shop with a list (otherwise you'll end up wasting money as well as time).

Don't let your pantry go bare. Replace food you run out of on your next shopping trip, instead of waiting until you need it and have to run to the store just for that item (and end up tempted to spend extra money on things you don't really need!). This is especially important if you are the type who never makes menu plans. If you do make menus ahead of time, they can be a help when it comes to both budgeting and making a shopping list.

Kitchen Efficiency

Organize your kitchen and make efficient use of the space you have—place items that you use often within easy reach; group items used for certain jobs, such as baking, together in one spot.

Keep your appliances out where you can use them easily and quickly. If you have to drag your food processor out of the cupboard every time you use it, you probably won't. Give away or sell appliances you never use, and gradually purchase the ones that will be of help to you. Really make use of the ones you decide to keep or purchase. Use that old pressure cooker to quick-cook beans for the freezer; resurrect that dusty slow-cooker for soups and spaghetti sauce.

If possible, double recipes and freeze some for a later date. It takes only minutes more to make a double batch of beans, spaghetti sauce, or soup.

To keep meals simple, make one interesting dish (such as a vegetable curry or stir-fry), and serve it with something simple (like rice and fruit). Other ideas on this theme might be: substantial soup or salad with bread; hummus with pita bread or crackers and raw vegetables; *Quick-Baked Potatoes* (p. 153) with whatever toppings you have around. Most of the recipes in this book can stand on their own as the main part of a meal.

Learn to cook, or more specifically, learn to cook properly. It's so much faster when you know how to slice quickly and efficiently. Use a large, sharp knife—I don't now how many times I've seen people struggling to chop onions with a dull paring knife! Quickly snip parsley and other herbs and dried fruits (even cut pizza) with kitchen scissors. Peel garlic by covering the clove with the flat side of a large knife and hitting the knife with your fist (the peel will split and come off easily). If you can't afford to take a cooking class, get a basic cooking video from your library.

Read the recipe through before you start!

Do as much advance preparation as possible for the next meal while you prepare another. Clean up as you go; rinse and reuse measuring utensils and pots. Keep a substitution, yield, and equivalent list of ingredients handy (*Joy of Cooking* has a good one).

Keep a kitchen notebook, noting down recipes that worked or changes you made, where to find certain recipes, good brand names of products, etc. Make notes in your cookbooks (use self-stick notes).

Check out the refrigerator daily, and make good use of leftovers in soups, salads, relish trays, bag lunches, etc.

About the Length of Time Needed to Make These Recipes

It is assumed that you know your way around a kitchen—if you don't, add a little more time. The time doesn't count answering phones, setting the table, comforting the baby, etc.

It is a given for these recipes that you either are handy with a chef's knife OR you have a food processor for chopping, mincing, and puréeing—also, that you have a blender.

Onions should be peeled and vegetables washed or even scrubbed. I call for frozen or pre-washed and trimmed fresh spinach, because washing spinach is very time-consuming.

Except for the baking recipes, you don't have to measure every spice or herb painstakingly—experienced cooks learn to "eyeball" amounts of ingredients, and, as you become more relaxed about this, cooking will be faster.

Remember that stoves and ovens differ—some are hotter and cook faster than others. Toaster ovens do not get as hot as ovens or oven broilers.

Equipment for the Time-Challenged Cook

Except for a blender, a food processor, sharp knives, and one good, nonstick skillet, you don't need any special equipment for this book. You will need a blender for many recipes, but it doesn't need to be a fancy, expensive one.

I recommend a food processor (again, it doesn't have to be an expensive one unless you plan to use it for bread dough), because it will save you a great deal of time and effort with chopping, and it works much better than a blender for thick mixtures.

You can buy a mini-processor very cheaply if all you need it for is chopping, and an inexpensive 3-speed blender with a glass container and a good motor is fine (10 speed buttons are totally unnecessary). But, if you can afford a mid-sized food processor, you'll find it endlessly useful for making thick bean purées, grinding crumbs, making thick tofu mixtures and pizza dough, and slushing frozen fruits into sherbet, to name just a few possibilities.

Go out and buy one good, nonstick skillet, if you don't already have one—preferably one with a 10- to 15-year (or even lifetime) guarantee on the coating. For some things, such as browning tofu, a lightly greased pan just does not work properly.

As you replace your pots, look into buying good-quality, nonstick varieties. Include some baking pans as well as sauté and saucepans—you can buy one at a time as you replace old pans. With these, you can bake and brown foods with no oil whatsoever.

I also like to have a couple of cast-iron skillets and pots, and two large, stainless steel pots for boiling noodles, making soup and soymilk, etc.

Besides basic cooking equipment and your favorite specialty cooking items, have one or two good colanders, at least one wire whisk (a tiny one is handy too), and several sizes of heat-resistant rubber scrapers for getting every last drop of food out of bowls, the blender, processors, jars, and pots. Invest in a good-quality garlic crusher and vegetable peeler. A timer (or even two) is a lifesaver when you are distracted. You may want other useful items for quick cooking, such as a collapsible metal steamer, an Oriental ginger grater, a salad spinner, a good can opener, kitchen scissors, a kitchen scale, a pasta rake, and a wok and lid.

Small electric appliances that I wouldn't want to be without are: a small electric coffee/spice grinder (I mince small amounts of garlic and fresh ginger, and it's fast and efficient for grinding raw cashews, flax, and sesame seeds, as well as spices); a toaster oven; an electric waffle iron/sandwich or pancake griddle; and a hand-held mixer. Some of my friends also swear by electric rice cookers, bread machines, and slow-cookers.

Pressure cookers: A pressure cooker is very handy to have. With a pressure cooker you can have unsoaked dried beans cooked in under an hour! Half a large winter squash cooks in 8 minutes, and you can pressure-steam potatoes for baking so that they are crisp-skinned and cooked in 25 minutes. Soups cook in minutes. Using covered stainless steel bowls or ceramic casseroles, steamer baskets, and foil packets,

you can cook several foods at once in a pressure cooker.

Newer pressure cooker models are made of stainless steel and have triple bottoms to prevent burning. Built-in safety valves eliminate the danger of food escaping while in use and make it impossible to open the pot while still under pressure. New valves allow pressure to drop within seconds when cooled under running water.

Once you have the pressure up and the heat turned down, you can set your timer (another important item) and prepare the rest of the meal.

Microwave ovens: For many years I refused to buy a microwave oven because of vague fears that they were somehow "dangerous." As a food writer, however, I felt obliged to investigate this very popular modern cooking device.

No microwave energy remains in the food, and microwaves are not remotely related to food irradiation or X-rays. This is a common and erroneous concern of many people, probably due to the word "radiation," which merely means emission of waves or particles. Anything that gives off energy or heat radiates.

We are exposed to EMFs (electromagnetic fields) from many electronic items in our homes these days, including microwave ovens. However, low-current items, such as electric blankets, pose more of a problem than microwave ovens do because they are used in close proximity for long periods of time.

New microwave ovens do not present leakage problems. Since 1971, microwave ovens have been required to have two independent interlock systems to stop microwave production the moment the latch is released or the door is opened, AND a monitoring system to stop the oven if either or both of the interlocks fail. Even stricter regulations came into effect in 1983. Models certified by Underwriters Laboratories (look for the UL mark) have undergone even more rigorous testing. In any case, microwave energy is contained within the oven and is generated for only short periods of time.

There ARE safety rules that should be followed, as with any heating or cooking device, and there are concerns about certain types of packaging, wrapping of foods, and cooking vessel materials. All of these problems are easily surmounted.

Follow the safety regulations that come with your microwave, clean around the door frame regularly, and use common sense, just as you would around your stove.

Plates and cooking vessels used in a microwave DO become hot, so use potholders and watch for steam just as you would cooking on a stove or in a regular oven. People scald themselves by spilling hot liquids or from the steam that is released when they open the covering of the food. Obviously, children should be supervised when using a microwave, just as they should when cooking on a stove. And don't heat baby bottles or baby food in a microwave, as they often become too hot too fast.

As for cooking and packaging materials, it is not necessary to buy commercial microwave-packaged foods or to use plastic containers.

I use microwave-safe bowls and plates, and Pyrex pie pans, as both cooking vessels and lids, and Pyrex 1- and 2-quart measuring beakers. If you use any plastic containers, use Tupperware, which is high-quality and proven to be microwave-safe. Don't use paper bags or cloth towels for cooking—get a microwave popcorn popper and, for soaking up moisture from foods, don't use paper towels made from recycled paper (they may contain metal).

While I rarely cook meals in a microwave oven, I do use it often for cooking certain vegetables. Broccoli, brussels sprouts, and asparagus, for instance, keep their lovely green color when microwaved, even when they are soft. A microwave is also useful for making sauces, puddings, gravies, popcorn, granola, croutons, no-fat potato and tortilla chips, crumb crusts, and for steps within recipes—like precooking onions or cooking a cornstarch sauce or gravy.

So, while a microwave oven is certainly not necessary, it can be a real effort- and time-saver for low-fat, vegetarian cooking. Cornell University researchers have also found that microwaving vegetables with very little water (1 tsp. for each 4 oz.) preserves 50%-100% of the nutrients (other methods preserve from 40%-60%). I have included microwave options wherever viable in recipes.

Convenience Foods and Meat Substitutes

For today's busy cooks, the use of commercial convenience foods is essential, but be cautious. Use breads, cereals, and crackers without added fats. Avoid products that are nothing more than fat-free junk food—full of sugar, salt, artificial flavors, sweeteners, fat substitutes, refined ingredients, and the like. Artificial sweeteners or fats are not recommended and not used in this book. They simply keep your taste buds clamoring for more sweet, greasy foods, and the jury is not in yet on whether or not these products may be harmful. Make use of quality commercial products like baked tortilla chips, fruit sorbets, and reduced-fat, non-dairy beverages and desserts, etc.

Naturally, I'd also like to mention some other convenience items, such as canned diced tomatoes, canned beans, and vegetarian broth cubes or powder; they are time savers you should always have on hand. Be aware that you often pay premium price for having someone else do the work for you—pick and choose your convenience items, using only what will really save you time and effort, or free you from a chore you really hate.

Check out:

Jars of minced garlic and ginger (often found in the Oriental foods section)

bags of frozen stir-fry vegetables, green peas and peas with carrots, corn, small whole green beans, and other vegetables that you use often

frozen spinach, both chopped and whole leaf

bags of washed and trimmed fresh spinach

roasted red peppers in a jar (these can actually be cheaper than fresh red peppers at certain times of the year and in certain areas)

frozen grated potatoes (without oil)

frozen bell pepper strips (all colors)

bottled lemon and lime juice (to use if you run out of fresh)

Fresh, packaged, prepared salad or stir-fry vegetables from the produce section can also be handy at times, but be aware that they can cost as much as 10 TIMES the price of regular vegetables, AND they lose nutrients very rapidly in this state. So consider preparing your own salads and using frozen stir-fry vegetables.

I mince fresh garlic and ginger quickly in my little electric spice grinder rather than buy them in jars. You can peel fresh ginger and keep chunks of it in a jar of dry sherry in the refrigerator for months, or buy Oriental pickled ginger in jars. You can mince a quantity of fresh garlic in your processor or spice grinder, place it in an airtight jar, cover it with oil, and keep it refrigerated for a week or two. You can buy sliced and chopped onions in some produce sections, but it takes so little time to do this in a food processor that I have never bought the prepared kind. Nor do I care for frozen or canned mushrooms, so I always use fresh.

Meat substitutes offend some vegetarians, but it's a matter of personal taste, not a moral issue. Very few of us were raised as vegetarians (and even fewer as vegans), so we are abandoning family memories and traditions along with our formerly favorite animal foods.

Some people are able to "throw off the old" with amazing speed, immediately adopting a simple, plant-based diet that bears no resemblance to what Mom served us. But most of us, I believe, adopt a "fusion" approach and never entirely give up the habit of using at least a few vegetarian foods that remind us of "the real thing," the so-called "transition" foods like veggie burgers.

This is a time-honored practice in China and Japan. In the Far East, Buddhist vegetarians have been refining their food for a thousand years, using tofu and other soyfoods, mushrooms, and wheat gluten to produce delectable vegetarian "duck," "pork," "chicken," "shrimp," and other "meats" used in their highly sophisticated cuisine. They invented meat substitutes so that people wouldn't kill animals, but could still enjoy the tastes and textures they had become accustomed to. If it saves our arteries and saves the animals, if it tastes good, AND it fills some more subtle needs, why shouldn't we do the same?

I go through stages where I eat mostly vegetables and beans as main courses, and at other times I enjoy stews, burgers, "meatballs," etc., that I make out of textured vegetable protein, tofu, seitan, yuba, and other vegetarian foods.

You'll find that these recipes are not, for the most part, dependent on meat substitutes—in many cases you can use mushrooms instead of seitan, or chick-peas instead of tofu, for example. The choice is yours—Just keep an open mind, and try some of these foods for yourself.

The Glossary on pps. 181-85 will give you information on foods that might be unfamiliar to you.

chapter II

homemade basics

Although none of the recipes in this chapter take much time or effort to make, most qualify as "staples" (generally dairy and meat substitutes) that should be made ahead of time in order to be ready to use at a moment's notice. If you are really pressed for time, you may prefer to buy these items ready-made. But I would like to give you the choice to make your own, since ready-made foods are generally expensive.

Most of these recipes keep well in the refrigerator or freezer. I usually make up a batch of whatever I'm running short of while I'm in the kitchen making something else that doesn't need my constant attention. Or, you can take an hour on a weekend to make up staples for the week.

NOTE: See the section on substituting ingredients if you have an allergy on pps. 13-15.

basic bean cooking

Many cooks don't mind cooking large pots of beans to freeze for future use when they are in the kitchen doing something else. Others object to having to deal with all those cans or to the price of canned beans compared to dry beans. In any case, all of the bean recipes in this book (except those using fast-cooking split red lentils) call for already cooked beans of some kind.

Beans can be cooked without soaking, but soaking and discarding the soaking water does alleviate some intestinal gas. The overnight soak is the best, if you remember to do it (use 3-4 cups water per cup of dry beans, and keep the beans in a cool place).

Quick-Soak Method: Use 3 cups water per 1 cup dry beans. Bring to a boil and simmer for 2 minutes. Remove from the heat, cover, and let stand for 1 hour.

Pressure-Soaking: Cook the beans under high pressure for 1 minute, using 4 cups water

for each 1 cup dry beans. Quick-release the pressure under cold running water.

Whichever soaking method you use, discard the soaking water, and add fresh liquid for cooking. The nutrient loss is minimal.

The Bean Cooking Chart on p. 25 gives cooking times for soaked, unsoaked, open-kettle, and pressure cooking methods. Whichever method you choose, cook the beans in plain water until the skins are soft, then add salt to taste and, if you wish, a bay leaf or two, a few whole peeled garlic cloves, a chopped onion, and maybe a sprig of thyme. These simple ingredients make a delicious pot of beans that can be used in other recipes or eaten alone for their own goodness. The flavored broths from chick-peas and soybeans are particularly delicious and can be used as vegetarian stock.

The pressure cooker is indispensable for spur-of-the-moment bean cooking. Some beans can be cooked without soaking in under 30 minutes! Follow the directions for your cooker.

The microwave does not significantly save time when cooking dry beans. Save it for recipes that start with cooked or canned beans, or for thawing or reheating beans.

quick-cooking frozen beans

Frozen soaked beans cook more quickly than regular soaked beans.

Use any method of soaking, discard the water, and place the beans in freezer containers. Cover with fresh water, allowing space for expansion, and freeze. They can be cooked later by either the stovetop or pressure cooking method. You should be able to cook them in about ¾ of the usual time.

super-quick red lentils

The "star" of quick-cook legumes is the split red lentil (Indian masoor dal). These tiny, orange-colored lentils have had their seed coats removed, so they cook without soaking in as little as 15-20 minutes (depending on age, size, and how they are to be served). You can cook them for 10 minutes, drain, and substitute them for white beans, chick-peas, etc. In pâtés, purées, soups, etc., the "Red Chief" red lentil is a new type that cooks in 5 minutes and holds its shape well, so it is good for salads.

storing frozen cooked beans

One 15-16 oz. can of beans contains about 1½ cups cooked beans. I freeze my home-cooked beans in containers of 1½ cups, 3 cups, or 4½ cups of beans so I can use them in recipes calling for so many cans of beans. If you use a microwave to thaw the beans, freeze them in microwave-safe containers. Otherwise, you can soften the beans by placing the container in a pot of hot water, then empty the contents into a colander (save the liquid if you like), and finish thawing by running hot tap water over the beans until they separate.

dehydrated beans

One cup dehydrated bean flakes (available in bulk in many natural food stores) soaked for 5 minutes in ¾ cup boiling water yields 1 cup mashed beans.

bean cooking times				
Use 3 cups of water for each cup of dried beans				
Bean	Soaked, open-kettle	No soak and pressure cook	Soak and pressure cook	Yield per 2 cups dry
Aduki	30 min.	15 min.	5-10 min.	6⅔
Anasazi	60 min.	25 min.	15 min.	5
Black	90 min.	30-35 min.	20 min.	5
Black-eyed peas	25 min.	10 min.	5-8 min.	4¾
Chick-pea (garbanzo)	4½ hrs.	35 min.	25 min.	5
Great Northern	90 min.	25 min.	20 min.	5
Kidney	35-40 min.	30 min.	15-20 min.	4½
Lentil, brown*	20-25 min.	**	**	5
Lentil, red*	15-20 min.	**	**	3⅓
Lima, baby	30 min.	10-15 min.	8 min.	4
Navy	35-40 min.	25 min.	15 min.	5
Pinto	90 min.	35-40 min.	20-25 min.	5
Soybeans	**	60 min.	45 min.	4
Split Peas*	75-90 min.	7 min.	**	4
* It is not necessary to presoak lentils and split peas ** Do not use this method for this variety of bean				

Adapted from *Fabulous Beans* by Barbara Bloomfield (Book Publishing Company: 1994)

about textured vegetable protein

Textured vegetable protein is a low-fat, dry product, used as a meat substitute. It is made from soy flour, cooked under pressure, then extruded to make different sizes and shapes. It has the advantage of being lower in fat than tofu and can take the place of frozen tofu in many recipes. Even if you object to the use of "meat substitutes" on a regular basis, textured vegetable protein can be a great transition food for people who were raised on meat and, despite the best of motives and intentions, miss their familiar foods and textures. I have had great success using textured vegetable protein in vegetarian foods for meat-loving teenagers.

Textured vegetable protein will keep for a long time, has no cholesterol, almost no fat and sodium, and is an excellent source of protein and fiber. It is easily rehydrated for use in soups, stews, casseroles, and sauces. The most common form available is granules, which have a ground meat-like texture. They are excellent in chilies and spaghetti sauces and can be made into burgers and "sausage" patties (p. 28). I use them in egg rolls and cabbage rolls too. Textured vegetable protein can also be found in the form of flakes and chunks. All these types can be ordered by mail (p. 186).

Reconstituted textured vegetable protein can be made ahead of time and refrigerated for several days, or frozen for future use. The granules are quickly rehydrated by mixing with almost an equal amount of boiling liquid, covering, and setting aside for 5 minutes. Boiling water is usually used for reconstituting, but broth or tomato juice can also be used. (I usually add 1 or 2 tablespoons of soy sauce and a sprinkling of sesame oil for flavor to each cup of textured vegetable protein.) The rule is, for each cup of textured vegetable protein granules, use ⅞ cup liquid (yields 1⅓ cups reconstituted).

The chunks take a little longer to reconstitute, but have an amazingly meat-like texture and a pleasant, mild taste. Different marinades can be used to vary the flavor. The chunks are excellent in stews and spicy sauces, stir-fries, and kabobs.

Reconstitute the chunks by mixing 1 cup of them with 2 cups water or broth in a saucepan, bringing them to a boil, then simmering for about 15 minutes, or until the chunks are tender but not mushy. Drain and squeeze off any excess liquid, especially if the chunks are to be marinated. One and one-half cups dry chunks yield about 2 cups reconstituted. The chunks will pick up the flavors in a spicy sauce or stew, but, for a more flavorful product, use a strong vegetarian broth for reconstituting. An easy flavorful broth is 3 cups water, 3 T. EACH ketchup and soy sauce, and 1 T. nutritional yeast. The addition of a little soy sauce and/or yeast extract (Marmite) will add a "beefy" taste. Freeze the reconstituted chunks on cookie sheets so that they remain separate, then store in plastic bags—this way you can measure out as much as you like and add directly to stews, sautés, or sauces without thawing. Alternatively, freeze the cooked chunks in their cooking liquid in amounts that you use frequently, then thaw them in the microwave. Textured vegetable protein chunks can be used in many recipes that call for chunks of tofu, tempeh, and seitan, if you don't like the taste and texture of those products, or if you are allergic to the wheat gluten in seitan.

vegetarian "ground pork"

Makes the equivilant of 1 lb. (8 to 10 patties)

1 c. dry textured vegetable protein granules
¾ c. boiling water
2 T. soy sauce
4 oz. reduced-fat, firm or medium-firm tofu, mashed
½ c. pure gluten powder (vital wheat gluten)

per patty: calories: 84, protein: 14 gm., fat: 1 gm., carbohydrates: 5 gm.

This is a very versatile mixture which I use uncooked for things such as won ton and other Oriental dumplings, egg rolls, etc.

In a medium bowl, mix together the textured vegetable protein, water, and soy sauce. Let this soak for about 5 minutes, then add the tofu and mix together well. Let the mixture cool thoroughly (if you don't, the gluten will clump into strings). To speed this up, you can spread the mixture on a plate, and place it in the freezer for a few minutes. Add the gluten powder and mix well with your hands.

To cook the mixture, form it into 8-10 thin patties. Steam the patties (or links) over simmering water for 20 minutes.

Microwave Method: Micro-steam the patties on a plastic microwave steamer in a covered bowl containing 1 c. water for about 5 minutes.

These firm up when cooled and can be browned immediately or later in a nonstick pan or on a grill, if you wish. Refrigerate or freeze for future use; you can also double or triple the recipe.

vegetarian "burger"

This mixture makes tasty "burgers" and is also useful as a substitute for cooked hamburger in many recipes.

Follow the recipe for Vegetarian "Ground Pork," but use 1 T. soy sauce and 1 T. yeast extract (Marmite) instead of the 2 T. soy sauce. Along with the tofu add 1 T. ketchup, 1 tsp. Kitchen Bouquet or Vegetarian Worcestershire Sauce (p. 77), 1 tsp. dried marjoram, ½ tsp. EACH garlic granules, onion powder, and dried thyme, and freshly ground black pepper to taste. Make into 8 patties. Steam and brown as directed.

vegetarian "sausage"

Make the Vegetarian "Ground Pork," adding along with the tofu: 2 tsp. crumbled sage leaves, 1 tsp. dried marjoram, ½ tsp. EACH garlic granules, onion powder, thyme, salt, and red pepper flakes, freshly ground black pepper to taste, and 1 tsp. liquid smoke (optional).

Make 10 thin patties or 20 small sausage "links," and cook according to either method as directed in the basic recipe, then brown on all sides on a grill or nonstick pan.

vegetarian "chorizo"

This spicy version is delicious with Spanish and Mexican foods.

Make the Vegetarian "Ground Pork," using only ½ cup boiling water and adding, along with the soy sauce: 2 T. red wine vinegar, 2 T. dry red wine, 1 T. EACH chile powder and paprika, 1 tsp. EACH salt, onion powder, and dried oregano, ½ tsp. EACH garlic granules and ground cumin, and ¼ tsp. ground cinnamon. Instead of ½ cup pure gluten powder, use only ¼ cup and add 2 T. unbleached flour with the tofu. Steam and brown as directed.

vegetarian Italian "sausage"

Make the Vegetarian "Ground Pork," using only ½ c. boiling water and adding along with the soy sauce: 2 T. red wine vinegar, 2 T. ketchup, 1 tsp. EACH dry basil, oregano, and onion powder, ½ tsp. dried red chile flakes, ¾ tsp. ground fennel or anise, ½ tsp. EACH dried thyme, salt, and garlic granules, and black pepper to taste. Form into 10-14 "links" and cook as directed.

Variation: For "sweet sausage," omit the chile flakes.

pan-fried "breast of tofu"

Makes 32 slices

BREAST OF TOFU MARINADE
1½ c. water
¼ c. soy sauce
3 T. nutritional yeast flakes
2 tsp. crumbled, dried sage leaves, or
   1 tsp. ground sage
½ tsp. dried rosemary
½ tsp. dried thyme
½ tsp. onion powder

1½-2 lbs. reduced-fat, extra-firm or
   pressed tofu

per slice: calories: 41, protein: 6 gm., fat: 1 gm., carbohydrates: 2 gm.

This is a staple in my house. I call it "breast of tofu," because it takes the place of chicken breast in sandwiches, stir-fries, salads, and many other dishes. I keep some marinating in the refrigerator at all times, to use at a moment's notice.

Prepare Breast of Tofu Marinade by combining the water, soy sauce, nutritional yeast, and spices in a 2-quart bowl.

Instead of all or some of the traditional "poultry seasonings" (thyme, sage, etc.), use cumin, coriander, basil, oregano, or whatever herbs are suitable for the dish you are making. For spicy *Breast of Tofu*, add as much Louisiana-style hot sauce to the marinade as you like.

Cut the tofu into ¼-inch thick slices. Marinate for as little as a few hours or as long as two weeks (in the refrigerator). Turn the slices, spoon over the marinade from time to time, or store in a tightly lidded container, and shake.

Simply pan-fry as many slices as you need in a nonstick pan over medium heat until browned on both sides. Use immediately or cool on racks and refrigerate. The wrapped slices will keep well in the refrigerator for several days or can be frozen for several weeks. Separate the slices with pieces of waxed paper for easy removal of just a few slices.

NOTE: See the quick marinating tip on the next page.

smoky pan-fried tofu

This variation is great for stir-fries, enchiladas, casseroles, etc. See the Kedegeree recipe on p. 165 for a spur-of-the-moment smoked tofu method.

Using half the tofu called for in *Breast of Tofu*, mix ¾ cup water, 2 T. soy sauce, and ½ tsp. liquid smoke together. (For a more pronounced smoky flavor, use ½ T. liquid smoke.) Pour over the tofu slices in a plastic container with a tight lid. Let marinate for at least 12 hours or several days.

Pan-fry as for *Breast of Tofu*.

Quick Marinating Tip: If you can't wait for this to marinate before using, simmer the tofu slices in the marinade in a nonstick or lightly oiled skillet over medium-high heat for 5 minutes, to allow some of the marinade to be absorbed quickly.

marinated tofu cubes

These have always been well-liked by novice tofu-users in my workshops. They make a great, low-fat alternative to feta cheese, and the drained cubes can be crumbled in salads or on pizza.

Cut firm (not pressed) tofu into small cubes, and cover them in a bowl or jar with your favorite fat-free commercial vinaigrette, using cider, rice, or white wine vinegar to avoid discoloration.

Cover the container and refrigerate for up to three weeks, shaking the mixture gently from time to time.

You can give jars of marinated tofu as gifts by packing the tofu into pint canning jars with springs of fresh herbs, whole dried chilies, and whole cloves of peeled garlic for decoration and flavoring. A jar of these makes a nice addition to a low-fat, vegan antipasto tray.

tofu mayonnaise

Makes 1⅓ cups

**1 (10.5 oz.) pkg. reduced-fat, extra-firm
    or firm SILKEN tofu
1½ T. cider vinegar or lemon juice
1 tsp. salt
½ tsp. dry mustard
⅛ tsp. white pepper
OPTIONAL: 1 tsp. sweetener of your
    choice**

per 2 tablespoons: calories: 13, protein: 2 gm.,
fat: 0 gm., carbohydrates: 1 gm.

*Silken tofu makes a smooth, thick, rich-tasting
mayonnaise that doesn't separate easily and
needs no oil.*

Combine all the ingredients in a blender
until very smooth. This will keep about 2
weeks in the refrigerator.

NOTE: Use either this recipe or the Low-Fat
Mayonnaise recipe on the next page as a base
for the flavored mayonnaise variations below.

Aioli: To make a garlic dip for cold, steamed
vegetables and artichokes, use lemon juice,
omit the mustard, and add 4 peeled garlic
cloves while blending. This also makes a good
spread for making garlic toast.

Tofu "Hollandaise": Use lemon juice
instead of vinegar, and omit the mustard. Use
soft silken tofu and heat gently just before serving. Add herbs such as dill, tarragon, or basil to
taste. For a tangier sauce, add ½ tsp. cumin and
a pinch of cayenne.

Tofu Tartar Sauce: Add ½ cup chopped
onion and ½ cup chopped dill pickle, with
some of the pickle brine to taste. If you have no
pickles, use chopped cucumber with dillweed
and white wine vinegar to taste.

Easy Coleslaw Dressing: Mix the basic Tofu
Mayonnaise with any kind of fruit juice until it
is thin enough and sweet enough to your taste.
You can flavor this with spices or herbs, if you
wish.

low-fat mayonnaise

Makes about 2 cups
(can be soy-free)

½ c. + 2 T. cold water

1 tsp. agar powder or 2 T. agar flakes

3 T. cornstarch or wheat starch (other starches don't work well)

1 c. reduced-fat soymilk OR other non-dairy milk

2 T. apple cider, white wine vinegar, or lemon juice

1½ tsp. salt

¾ tsp. dry mustard

pinch white pepper (or some lemon pepper to taste)

¼ c. extra-virgin olive oil (no substitutes)

per 2 tablespoons: calories: 42, protein: 0 gm., fat: 2 gm., carbohydrates: 3 gm.

For those who do not like tofu mayonnaise or the commercial "light" mayos (most are not vegan, anyway), here is a delicious solution! It contains a small amount of oil, but 1 tablespoon has only about 1.8 gm. fat, in comparison with "light" mayonnaise, which contains 5 gm. per tablespoon, and real mayo, which contains about 11 gm. per tablespoon.

In a small cup, soak the agar in the water for a few minutes. In a small saucepan, stir together the cornstarch and dissolved agar over high heat until thick and translucent—not white.

Microwave Option: Place the above ingredients in a bowl, and microwave on HIGH for 30 seconds. Whisk. Repeat 3 times, or until very thick and translucent—not white.

Place the cornstarch mixture and all other ingredients, EXCEPT the oil, in a blender or food processor. Blend well, then add the oil slowly through the top while the machine is running. Blend until the mixture is very white, frothy, and emulsified (you can't see any oil globules). Pour into a clean jar, cover, and refrigerate. Keeps several weeks.

bright idea

This mayonnaise and its variations can be used as a savory vegetable and toast topping.
You can make this with any non-dairy milk.

Tartar Sauce: To the chilled mayonnaise, add ¾ c. minced raw onion and ¾ c. minced dill pickle. Add pickle brine to taste, if you wish. If you have no pickles, use chopped cucumber with dillweed and white wine vinegar to taste.

Russian Dressing: This dressing is a traditional addition to many deli sandwiches. To 1 c. of either mayonnaise, add 1 T. prepared horseradish, 1 tsp. *Vegetarian Worcestershire Sauce* (p. 77), ¼ c. chile sauce, and 1 tsp. grated onion.

Soy-Free Sour Cream: Follow the recipe for *Low-Fat Mayonnaise*, using plain rice milk or other soy-free, non-dairy "milk." Omit the vinegar, mustard powder, and olive oil. Instead, use 2 T. + 2 tsp. lemon juice and ⅓ c. cashew butter (or ¼ c. ground raw cashews). Use only ½ tsp. salt. (This recipe contains less than 1 gm. of fat per T.) Makes 2 cups.

Flavored Mayonnaise: Flavored mayonnaise can turn a quick sandwich or salad meal into a gourmet treat. Try these suggestions and then invent your own.

When making either *Tofu Mayonnaise* (p. 31) or *Low-Fat Mayonnaise* (p. 32):

1) Use cranberry or other berry vinegar, balsamic or sherry vinegar, or lime juice instead of ordinary vinegar or lemon juice.
2) Use your favorite herbal vinegar plus 3 to 4 T. of the appropriate fresh herb.

Or add to already prepared *Tofu Mayonnaise*, *Low-Fat Mayonnaise*, or your favorite reduced-fat commercial mayonnaise:

3 T. minced pickled jalapeños
3 minced chile chipotles
several T. *Pesto* (p. 77), pureéd roasted red pepper, pureéd soaked sun-dried tomato, or mashed roasted garlic
1 T. minced or grated fresh gingerroot
2 T. prepared horseradish
1 T. curry powder
¼ c. or more minced fresh herbs, such as basil, mint, oregano, cilantro, tarragon, etc. (with or without a clove of garlic)
⅓ c. chopped chives, 1 T. grated lemon zest, and Louisiana hot sauce to taste (for a "Creole" mayonnaise)
1 T. Chinese hoisin sauce (or ½ T. EACH dark or red miso and honey or alternate)
¼-½ c. salsa
1-2 tsp. wasabi powder (Japanese green horseradish)
2 T. grated lemon, lime, orange, or grapefruit zest
¼-⅓ c. minced Japanese-style pink pickled ginger
3-6 T. of your favorite chutney
12-18 cloves (1 head) roasted garlic (see p. 44 for a quick version)
(You can also use these flavoring ideas with *Tofu Cream Cheeze Spread*, p. 36)

You can also make tasty sandwich spreads by mixing together half *Tofu* or *Low-Fat Mayonnaise* and half grainy gourmet or creamy Dijon mustard (for a "Dijonnaise"), or light soy or chick-pea miso.

tofu "ricotta cheese"

Makes 1 generous cup

**8 oz. reduced-fat, medium-firm tofu,
    mashed and drained**
3 T. reduced-fat soymilk
¼ tsp. salt

Mix all the ingredients together in a bowl, and refrigerate.

NOTE: This recipe works best with very fresh tofu.

per ¼ cup: calories: 61, protein: 6 gm., fat: 3 gm., carbohydrates: 3 gm.

tofu "cottage cheese"

Makes about 2½ cups

**1 lb. reduced-fat, medium-firm tofu,
    mashed coarsely and drained**
**½ (10.5 oz.) box reduced-fat, extra-firm
    SILKEN tofu**
1 T. lemon juice
¾ tsp. salt
¼ tsp. sugar or other sweetener

This is delicious with chives and/or chopped vegetables, or with pineapple tidbits.

Sprinkle ½ tsp. of the salt on the mashed tofu in a medium bowl. In a blender or food processor, mix the silken tofu, remaining salt, sugar, and lemon juice until VERY smooth. Scoop into the bowl with the mashed tofu, and mix gently. Refrigerate.

per ¼ cup: calories: 52, protein: 6 gm., fat: 2 gm., carbohydrates: 2 gm.

dairy-free spreads

Butter substitutes are a problem. Dairy-free and natural spreads (margarines) can be very tasty, but they generally contain the same amount of fat as butter (a whopping 11 gm. per tablespoon!), so, if you use them, do so very sparingly and ONLY where they really matter to you.

Diet spreads contain about half as much fat, but most are not dairy-free, have a greasy mouth-feel, and little flavor. (Some also contain gelatin, an animal product, as do many of the new, no-fat spreads.) Check out what is available in your area (reading the labels carefully), or try using *Tofu Cream Cheeze Spread* and variations (p. 36).

Tofu Mayonnaise or *Low-Fat Mayonnaise* (and variations) can be used as a savory vegetable, bread, or toast topping or spread. *On-The-Spot Creamy "Butter" Sauce* (p. 74) is another possibility.

tofu sour cream

Makes 1 cup

1 (10.5 oz.) box reduced-fat, extra-firm SILKEN tofu

2 T. lemon juice

½ tsp. sugar or alternate sweetener

¼ tsp. salt

per 2 tablespoons: calories: 17, protein: 3 gm., fat: 0 gm., carbohydrates: 1 gm.

Silken tofu makes a smooth, rich-tasting mixture which can be used anywhere you would normally use sour cream, including cooking.

Process in a food processor or blender until VERY smooth. Keep in a covered container in the refrigerator for up to a week.

For a topping for fruit, sweeten the "sour cream" with a tablespoon or two of liquid sweetener, fruit-sweetened jam or jelly, fruit juice concentrate, and/or fruit liqueur.

Tofu Yogurt: Reduce the salt to a small pinch, and use up to 4 T. of lemon juice. If it seems too thick, thin with some water to make it the consistency you prefer. (There are several brands of soy yogurt now available in health food stores, but I prefer this for sauces and cooking.)

NOTE: For a slightly richer "sour cream," see *Tofu-Cashew Sour Cream*, on p. 36.

tofu cream cheeze spread

Makes ⅞ cup

1 (10.5 oz.) box reduced-fat, extra-firm SILKEN tofu, squeezed in a towel

1 oz. (about 3 T.) cashew butter, or 4 T. raw cashews, finely ground

4 tsp. lemon juice

½ tsp. salt

OPTIONAL: 1 tsp. liquid sweetener

per 2 tablespoons: calories: 83, protein: 7 gm., fat: 5 gm., carbohydrates: 4 gm.

This is one of the few recipes in which I use nuts, but 1 oz. of cashew butter mixed with low-fat silken tofu still yields a very low-fat product with wonderful richness and mouth-feel.

NOTE: You should use a food processor for this recipe, as it may be too thick for a blender.

Place the tofu in a clean tea towel, gather the end up, and twist and squeeze for a couple of minutes to extract most of the water. Crumble into the processing bowl of a food processor with the remaining ingredients, and process for several minutes until the mixture is VERY smooth. (You may have to stop the machine and loosen the mixture with a spatula once or twice.) Use right away or scrape it into a covered container and refrigerate. It firms up with refrigeration. (If you can't eat soy, see *Soy-Free Cream Cheeze*, p. 38)

Tofu-Cashew Sour Cream: This is richer than *Tofu Sour Cream* (p. 35), but still has only 1.8 gm. fat in 2 T. (Real sour cream contains 6 gm. fat in 2 T.)

Follow the above directions for *Tofu Cream Cheeze Spread*, but don't squeeze the tofu. Use 2 T. lemon juice, and add ⅓ c. soymilk. Process until very smooth and refrigerate. Makes 1¾ cups.

(If you can't eat soy, see *Soy-Free Sour Cream*, p. 33.)

Tofu Devonshire Cream: Use this on scones and other breads, or as a thick whipped cream substitute.

Make the basic *Tofu Cream Cheeze Spread*, but don't squeeze the tofu. Use only ¼ tsp. salt, and add 1 T. liquid sweetener.

Tofu-Miso "Goat Cheese" Spread: Make the basic *Tofu Cream Cheeze Spread* (squeezing the tofu), using only 2 tsp. of lemon juice, no salt (and no liquid sweetener). Add 2 T. light miso.

You may also add fresh or dried herbs, reconstituted dried tomatoes (see p. 46), roasted peppers, garlic, etc.

---

savory, gourmet tofu cream cheeze spreads

Use any of the flavor variations under *Flavored Mayonnaise* (p. 33) with the *Tofu Cream Cheeze Spread* and *Tofu "Goat Cheese" Spread* recipes to make gourmet cream cheeze spreads. Try also mixing one recipe with ½ c. of your favorite chutney for a spicy cracker spread.

sweet tofu cream cheeze spreads

I don't like these very sweet, but, if you prefer, you can add 1 T. maple syrup, or other favorite liquid sweetener to any of the fruit mixtures. Use one recipe Tofu Cream Cheeze Spread *as the basic mixture in each of these variations.*

Pineapple Spread: Add to the basic *Tofu Cream Cheeze Spread:* ½ tsp. vanilla, ¼ tsp. powdered ginger, and ¼ tsp. coconut extract (optional). Stir in (do not process) ½ c. squeezed and packed-down, unsweetened, crushed pineapple.

Fruit and Spice Spread (my favorite): Add to the basic *Tofu Cream Cheeze Spread:* ⅓ c. raisins, dried currants, chopped dried dates, prunes, figs, or any other dried fruit of your choice; ¾ tsp. vanilla; and ¼ tsp. cinnamon. You can add ¼ tsp. lemon or orange extract, if you like. Process until the fruit is finely chopped.

Banana or Apple Spread: Same as for Fruit and Spice Spread, but omit dried fruit and add ¼ c. mashed ripe banana OR thick, drained applesauce. With the banana addition, you can add ¼ tsp. coconut or peanut butter flavoring, if you like. Process until smooth.

Apricot-Orange Spread: Add to the *Tofu Cream Cheeze Spread:* 3 T. chopped dried apricots, ½ T. frozen orange juice concentrate, and a heaping ¼ t. ground coriander. Process until the fruit is well-chopped.

soy-free cream cheeze

Makes a scant 1½ cups
(soy-free)

1 c. unflavored non-dairy "milk"
scant 3 T. quick oats
3 T. raw cashew butter (or ¼ c. raw
cashews, finely ground in a
coffee/spice grinder)
½-1 T. cornstarch (depending upon how
soft you want it)
1 tsp. lemon juice
⅛-¼ tsp. salt

per 2 tablespoons: calories: 33, protein: 1 gm.,
fat: 1 gm., carbohydrates: 4 gm.

In a blender, mix ½ c. of the "milk" and the oatmeal until the mixture is fairly smooth. Add the rest of the ingredients. Blend until VERY smooth. Pour the mixture into a small saucepan, and whisk constantly over medium-high heat until it is thick and smooth.

MICROWAVE OPTION: Microwave the mixture in a medium-sized microwave-safe bowl or glass measuring beaker, covered with a plate, on HIGH for 1½ minutes. Whisk well, then cook on HIGH for another 2 minutes. Whisk again.)

Scrape the mixture into a hard plastic container with a lid, and refrigerate.

You can follow the flavoring suggestions for *Tofu Cream Cheeze Spread* (p. 36), or add some fresh herbs, garlic, etc.

homemade non-dairy "milks" and cereal toppings

Even though there are so many delicious, reduced-fat, non-dairy beverages on the market, you might like to try some of these toppings. They are certainly handy when you run out of your usual beverage, and cheaper too.

It's also a good idea to keep some instant light tofu beverage mix or other instant non-dairy milk powder on hand for emergencies. Made double-strength, these make good "cream" for cereals and hot drinks.

tofu milk

Makes 2 quarts

1 (10.5) oz. box reduced-fat, firm or extra-firm SILKEN tofu, crumbled
3 c. cold water
1 c. cold water
3-4 T. sweetener of your choice
OPTIONAL: 1½ tsp. vanilla extract, or ½ tsp. almond or coconut extract
¾ tsp. salt
enough cold water to make 2 quarts

per cup: calories: 40, protein: 3 gm., fat: 0, gm. carbohydrates: 6 gm.

Since making your own soymilk can be time-consuming, I've devised an easy and delicious alternative which is still much cheaper than commercial, non-dairy beverages (and usually less expensive than dairy milk too, depending upon where you live). It takes only minutes to make in your blender and can be used in cooking and baking.

In a blender, combine the tofu and 3 cups water until very smooth. Add 1 cup water, sweetener, vanilla, and salt, and blend again. Pour this into a 2-quart container, and add the rest of the water to make 2 quarts.

Stir well, pour into sterilized quart bottles, cap tightly, and refrigerate. Shake before pouring, as it tends to separate. This will keep about a week in the refrigerator.

pourable non-dairy cream

Makes 1 cup
(can be soy-free)

½ c. crumbled reduced-fat SILKEN tofu
½ c. commercial reduced-fat non-dairy
    milk
4-6 tsp. light sugar or maple syrup
¼ tsp. coconut extract (this doesn't
    make it taste like coconut, but gives
    the cream a rich flavor)
OPTIONAL: pinch salt

per 2 tablespoons: calories: 19, protein: 1 gm.,
fat: 0 gm., carbohydrates: 3 gm.

If you use soft silken tofu, this is like a cereal cream. If you use firm or extra-firm silken tofu, it will be like a thick pouring cream for puddings or desserts. For a cream that has no discernible soy flavor, use commercial low-fat rice or almond milk.

Place all the ingredients in a blender or food processor, and process until very smooth. Place in a covered container, and refrigerate for several hours, or overnight, before using.
To Make Soy-Free: Use cooked short grain brown rice instead of tofu.

low-fat coconut milk

Makes 1 cup
(can be soy-free)

¼ c. reduced-fat, firm or extra-firm
    SILKEN tofu
¾ c. commercial low-fat rice or almond
    milk (don't use soymilk—it doesn't
    work with this recipe)
½ tsp. coconut extract

per cup: calories: 64, protein: 5 gm., fat: 1 gm.,
carbohydrates: 9 gm.

This tastes deliciously rich and can be used in East Indian, West Indian, Southeast Asian, and other dishes which call for coconut milk (the real thing contains from 45 to 60 gm. of fat PER CUP!).

Blend until very smooth. Refrigerate.
To Make Soy-Free: Use cooked short grain rice instead of tofu.
Coconut Cream or Thick Coconut Milk: Use ½ c. of the silken tofu or cooked rice and ½ c. of the rice or almond milk. For a thinner milk, omit the tofu or rice, and use 1 c. rice or almond milk.

plain rice milk

Makes about 1 quart
(soy-free)

2 c. water
1 c. short grain brown rice
2 c. hot water

per cup: calories: 108, protein: 2 gm., fat: 0 gm.,
carbohydrates: 23 gm.

If you cannot use soymilk, there are commercial rice beverages for drinking and cold cereal. However, you may find them too expensive to use in cooking. This easy-to-make rice milk is excellent for use in gravies, sauces, and creamed soups, adding body and richenss without fat.

Bring 2 c. of water to a boil in a medium saucepan. Add 1 c. uncooked short grain brown rice, return to a boil, reduce heat, and simmer for 45 minutes. Combine the well-cooked rice and 2 c. hot water in a blender until very smooth.

The mixture will be thicker than dairy milk or soymilk, but may be thinned a bit with more water, if desired. It will thicken further when chilled. Store in a tightly covered, sterilized jar in the refrigerator, and shake well before using. This only keeps for 2 or 3 days.

banana milk

Makes 2 servings
(soy-free)

1 ripe banana, peeled and chunked
1 c. very cold water or fruit juice
½ tsp. vanilla, or ¼ tsp. almond or
    coconut extract

Process all the ingredients in a blender until very smooth. Use this immediately over cereal.

per serving: calories: 53, protein: .5 gm., fat: 0 gm.,
carbohydrates: 12 gm.

melty pizza cheeze

Makes 1¼ cups
(soy-free)

1 c. water
¼ c. nutritional yeast
2 T. cornstarch
1 T. flour
1 tsp. lemon juice
½ tsp. salt
¼ tsp. garlic granules
OPTIONAL: **4 tsp. calcium carbonate**
        powder
2 T. water
OPTIONAL: **1 T. canola oil**

per ¼ cup: calories: 37, protein: 3 gm., fat: 0 gm.,
carbohydrates: 6 gm.

This easy recipe is tastier than any commercial vegan cheese substitute and much cheaper. It makes great grilled cheese sandwiches and Quesadillas (p. 120) and can be used to make Golden Cheeze Sauce (p. 72). The optional added calcium carbonate powder gives 2 T. of the cheeze about the same amount of calcium as 1 oz. of dairy cheese. The nutritional yeast adds protein and lots of B-complex vitamins.

Place all the ingredients, except the water and optional oil, in a blender, and blend until smooth. Pour the mixture into a small saucepan and stir over medium heat until it starts to thicken, then let it bubble for 30 seconds. Whisk vigorously.

Microwave Option: Pour the mixture into a microwave proof bowl; cover and cook on HI for 2 minutes. Whisk, then microwave for 2 more minutes, and whisk again.

Whisk in the water and optional oil. The oil adds richness and helps it melt better, but the cheeze still only contains 2.6 gm. of fat per ¼ cup.

Drizzle immediately over pizza or other food, and broil or bake until a skin forms on top. Alternatively, refrigerate in a small, covered plastic container for up to a week. It will become quite firm when chilled but will still remain spreadable. You can spread the firm cheese on bread or quesadillas for grilling, or heat it to spread more thinly on casseroles, etc.

Melty Jack Cheeze: Omit the oil and add 1 T. tahini to the blender mixture.

Melty Suisse Cheeze: Omit the oil and use only ¼ tsp. salt. Add 1 T. tahini and 1 T. light soy or chick-pea miso to the blended mixture.

Melty Chedda' Cheeze: Use ⅓ c. nutritional yeast flakes and add ¼ tsp. EACH sweet Hungarian paprika and mustard powder. Use only ¼ tsp. salt and add 1 T. light soy or chick-pea miso to the blended mixture.

Smoky Cheeze: To the basic recipe or any of the above variations, add ⅛ tsp. liquid smoke.

Cheeze Sauce, Rarebit, or Fondue: Add 1-1¼ c. non-dairy milk, dry white wine, or beer (can be non-alcoholic) to any of the cheeze variations. (Try using the Suisse for fondue and the Chedda' for Rarebit.) You may add a pinch of nutmeg and white pepper. Add salt to taste.

Nacho Sauce: You can add drained, canned black beans, chopped jalapeños or other chiles, chopped olives, a pinch of cumin, etc., using Jack or Chedda' as a base.

quick-roasted (caramelized) garlic and onions

It usually takes 1½ to 2 hours to roast garlic (or onions) in the oven so that they are very tender, browned (or caramelized), and creamy. They can be used as a spread on toast or as an addition to soups (add the onions to rich vegetarian broth for French onion soup), salad dressings, and sauces. However, you can "cheat" and precook the garlic or onion by simmering in broth, then quick-browning in a non-stick skillet. If you like, make it up in quantity and refrigerate for later use.

Combine as many peeled cloves of garlic or diced or sliced peeled onions as you like with vegetarian broth or water in a saucepan. Use about ¼ c. of liquid for each 2 large heads (about 24 cloves) of garlic, or 2 medium onions. Bring the liquid to a boil, then cover and simmer over low heat for 10 minutes, or until soft.

To brown, place the soft garlic or onion in a nonstick skillet, and steam-fry over high heat, stirring constantly and adding just a bit of liquid (water, low-salt vegetarian broth, or dry wine diluted with water) at a time to keep it moving. Let the juices brown a little before adding the liquid each time. Use the liquid to scrape up the browned juices and distribute them among the contents of the pan. (You can add a teaspoon or so of brown sugar, Sucanat, or maple syrup if you want a sweeter caramelized flavor.) When the garlic or onions are browned to your satisfaction (this takes 5-10 minutes), let the remaining liquid cook away, and remove from heat.

roasted or grilled peppers

You can buy jars of roasted red peppers in supermarkets now, and the quality of these is very good. In some areas, and at some times of the year, red peppers are actually cheaper to buy this way than fresh, and they are certainly cheaper than those little jars of pimientos (which are just red peppers, after all). Feel free to use these when I call for roasted or grilled peppers in my recipes.

However, if you want to roast or grill your own, it's not hard. Seed and cut the peppers into halves, quarters, squares, or slices. Toss with a garlicky, no-fat vinaigrette dressing, and grill or broil on racks about 4" from the heat source for about 10 minutes total, or until they start to brown and become tender. I love them this way, with the skin on. To make real roasted peppers, blacken them over hot coals or flames, place in paper bags for 15 minutes to soften, and then peel the blackened skins off. (You can do this in a broiler, very close to the heat, or with a barbecue fork over an open gas flame.) This step is optional for the purposes of this book, because it takes extra time and effort.

seasoned coating mix

Makes 1⅓ cups
(soy-free)

1 c. soft whole wheat bread crumbs or finely crumbled, whole grain cold cereal
¼ c. cornmeal
2 tsp. paprika
1 tsp. salt (herbal or seasoned, if desired)
½ tsp. black pepper
½ tsp. ground sage
½ tsp. dried thyme
½ tsp. dried basil

Mix all the ingredients together, and store in a tightly covered container in the refrigerator.

breaded slices

Dip tofu, vegetable, or seitan slices in 1 c. reduced-fat soymilk mixed with 1 T. lemon juice. Dredge in Seasoned Coating Mix. Place on greased, dark cookie sheets, and bake at 400°F until golden on the bottom. Turn the slices over and bake until golden on the other side. This coating mixture is useful for tofu slices, sliced, oven-baked vegetables, (such as zucchini or eggplant), and seitan cutlets. Keep some ready for use in your refrigerator.

quick soaking dried mushrooms and dried tomatoes

You can quick-soak dried mushrooms and dried tomatoes, instead of soaking them in boiling water for 30 minutes, by covering them with hot water (or vegetarian broth for tomatoes) and simmering them for 10 minutes.

You can also quick-soak dried mushrooms and dried tomatoes in a microwave. Cover 4 dried mushrooms with water in a medium bowl, cover, and microwave 5 minutes. Let stand 5 minutes. Cover 4 dried tomatoes with vegetarian broth in a medium bowl. Cover and microwave 2 minutes. Let cool in the broth.

(See p. 181 about dried mushrooms.)

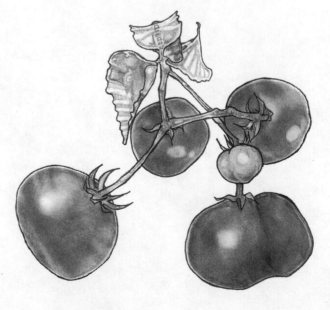

quick dips, spreads & drinks

When we're really on the run, all we may have time for is a blender beverage and/or crackers with a spread or raw vegetables with a dip. That spread often used to be peanut butter for many vegetarians, and the spreads or dips were usually based on high-fat mayonnaise, sour cream, and/or cream cheese. Now we turn more readily to low-fat bean spreads and vegetable dips made with tofu or beans. There are some good commercial varieties available now, but you can make your own very inexpensively and easily at home, especially if you keep some tofu and dehydrated bean flakes or canned beans on hand (or home-cooked beans in the freezer—see p. 23).

vegetable dip

Makes 1½ cups
(can be soy-free)

1 (10.5 oz.) box reduced-fat, extra-firm
   SILKEN tofu
2 T. lemon juice
½ (1½ oz.) packet vegetable soup mix
¼ tsp. salt

per ¼ cup: calories: 51, protein: 6 gm., fat: 2 gm., carbohydrates: 3 gm.

Don't use a soup mix that contains potatoes in this dip, or it will be too thick and gloppy.

Mix all the ingredients in a blender or food processor until smooth. Place in a bowl, cover, and refrigerate. Serve with crackers, no-fat baked potato chips, or raw vegetables.

Onion Dip: Use half a packet of vegetarian onion soup mix instead of the vegetable soup mix.

Soy-Free Vegetable Dip: Use 1½ c. *Low-Fat Mayonnaise* (p. 32) instead of tofu, salt, and lemon juice (check soup package labels for soy content).

classic spinach dip in a bread crust

Makes 12 servings
(can be soy-free)

Double recipe of *Vegetable Dip* (above)
1 (10 oz.) pkg. frozen chopped spinach,
   thawed and squeezed dry
2 green onions, chopped
1 (8 oz.) can water chestnuts, drained
   and chopped
OPTIONAL: **1 T. soy bacon chips**
1 large round pumpernickel or whole
   wheat French bread loaf

per serving: calories: 136,protein: 8 gm., fat: 2 gm., carbohydrates: 21 gm.

In a medium bowl, stir together the dip, spinach, green onions, water chestnuts, and optional soy bacon chips. Cover and refrigerate until serving time. (To thaw frozen spinach quickly, microwave in the box on high for 5 minutes, or thaw in a colander, unwrapped, under hot running water.)

Cut a slice off the top of the bread loaf, and scoop out a large hollow in the loaf. Fill with the dip. Cut the discarded bread into cubes, and serve with the dip and raw vegetable dippers.

Variation: Instead of using a hollowed-out loaf of bread to hold the dip, use a large, hollowed-out red cabbage. (Save the insides for salad or a cooked vegetable dish.) Serve with pita or bagel chips, baked potato chips, and raw vegetable dippers.

tofu-miso pâté

Makes ⅞ cup

1 (10.5 oz.) box reduced-fat, extra-firm SILKEN tofu
2 T. chopped fresh parsley
1½ T. light miso
½ green onion, chopped
½ T. tahini
1 tsp. dry dillweed
1 small clove garlic, peeled
pinch of nutmeg

per 2 tablespoons: calories: 58, protein: 5 gm., fat: 2 gm., carbohydrates: 3 gm.

This recipe is like a rich cream-cheese herb spread. It contains about 1.5 gm. fat per 2 tablespoons (compared to 10 gm. in real cream cheese!).

Place the tofu in a clean tea towel, gather the ends, and twist for a couple of minutes to squeeze out most of the water. Crumble the tofu into the processing bowl of a food processor with the remaining ingredients, and process until smooth. Pack into a bowl or container, cover, and refrigerate. Serve on crackers, rye crisp, toast, raw celery sticks, etc.

spicy bean dip or "refried" beans

Makes 3½ to 4 cups
(soy-free)

**3 (15 oz.) cans, or 4½ c. cooked plain
   beans, drained
1 small onion, minced
2 T. cider vinegar or wine vinegar
1 tsp. salt
1 tsp. ground cumin
1 tsp. dried oregano
3 cloves garlic, crushed, or 1 tsp. garlic
   granules
1 tsp. chile powder with hot red pepper
   sauce to taste and a few dashes of
   liquid smoke,
   or 2 tsp. chipotle chile**

per ¼ cup: calories: 80, protein: 4 gm., fat: 0 gm.,
carbohydrates: 15 gm.

This fat-free dip gets its light texture from being whirled for several minutes in the food processor. It can be made with black, red, or pinto beans, pinto or black bean flakes, or, in a pinch, red lentils cooked for 10 minutes. Good hot or cold, it makes a great stand-in for refried beans.

Place all the ingredients in a food processor, and blend for several minutes until very smooth. Place in a serving bowl, cover, and refrigerate. If you like, heat the dip in the microwave on high for about 3 minutes, or in a skillet (stirring constantly) until heated through. Serve with baked tortilla chips.

Variation: To use bean flakes instead of cooked or canned beans, pour 3¼ c. boiling water over 4½ c. bean flakes, cover, and let sit 5 minutes. Blend with all the other ingredients.

lentil "butter"

Makes 2 cups
(soy-free)

**¾ c. split red lentils
2 c. vegetarian broth
¼ c. water
½ tsp. dried thyme
½ tsp. dried basil**

per ¼ cup: calories: 50, protein: 3 gm., fat: 0 gm.,
carbohydrates: 9 gm.

Cooked, the red split lentils have a smooth, "buttery" taste. Use other fresh herbs for variety. Try this on toast or crackers, or use leftovers to make an instant soup, watered down with broth, water, or vegetable juice.

Rinse and drain the lentils, then cook with the broth and water for 15-20 minutes, or until soft. Purée the lentils in a blender or food processor, along with the herbs, until smooth. The mixture will be soupy, but will be spreadable after chilling. You can add garlic or onion, if you like.

low-fat hummus with a kick

Makes about 2½ cups
(soy-free)

**2 c. canned or well-cooked chick-peas,
    drained**
⅓ c. lemon juice, preferably fresh
1 T. tahini
4-6 cloves garlic, peeled
1 tsp. salt
½ tsp. ground cumin
pinch of cayenne
**OPTIONAL: 2 T. minced fresh herbs,
    and/or ¼ c. minced fresh parsley**

per ¼ cup: calories: 67, protein: 3 gm., fat: 1 gm.,
carbohydrates: 11 gm.

*The kick is from cumin, cayenne, plenty of
lemon, and lots of garlic. A tiny bit of tahini
gives just the right hint of sesame without over-
whelming the other flavors.*

Place everything in the food processor, and
blend for several minutes until smooth, adding
a bit of water so that it isn't too thick. (The
hummus will thicken with refrigeration.) Place
in a serving bowl, cover tightly with plastic
wrap, and refrigerate.

Serve with a platter of pita bread triangles
or crisps, rye crisp crackers, or slices of French
bread, and raw vegetables.

Green Hummus: Use 1½ tsp. salt, 1 tsp.
cumin, and ¼ tsp. cayenne. After blending
until smooth, add 1 (10 oz.) package frozen
chopped spinach, thawed and squeezed dry.
Blend again.

Bean Hummus: Use red lentils cooked 10
minutes, or try canned or cooked white (navy)
beans, white kidney (cannellini) beans, fava
beans, lima beans, lentils, or even black beans!

white bean pâté

Makes about 1½ cups
(soy-free)

1 large onion, minced
2 cloves garlic, minced
½ c. vegetable broth
1 (15 oz.) can white beans (white
kidney, cannellini, Great Northern,
or navy), drained (1½ c. cooked)
3 T. white wine vinegar or fresh lemon
juice
2 T. minced fresh parsley
½ tsp. salt
¼ tsp. EACH dried thyme and savory, or
other favorite herbs
white pepper to taste

per ¼ cup: calories: 77, protein: 4 gm., fat: 0 gm.,
carbohydrates: 15 gm.

I don't know why, but there's something so sophisticated about a white bean dip! Serve this warm or at room temperature with rye crisp crackers, pita or bagel crisps, slices of fresh or toasted French bread or breadsticks, and raw vegetable dippers such as carrot sticks, strips of bell pepper of any color, broccoli, etc.

Steam-fry the onion and garlic, using the broth as the liquid, until they are soft and as browned as you like them. (Browned onions give the dish a rich flavor.) Add the remaining ingredients to the skillet, and mash them with a potato masher. If you're serving the spread warm, stir it around until it is quite hot, then mound into a serving bowl, and serve immediately.

If you're serving it cold, don't bother mashing—just add the onions and other ingredients into a food processor, and process for several minutes so that the mixture is light. Mound into a serving bowl, and refrigerate until serving time, up to 3 days.

Variation: Use only 1½ T. lemon juice or vinegar, and add ¼ c. dried tomatoes, reconstituted and drained (p. 46), or ½ c. rinsed roasted red peppers. Process the mixture in the food processor until smooth.

quick, simple dips

Start with *Tofu Sour Cream* (p. 35), *Tofu-Cashew Sour Cream* (p. 35), *Soy-Free Sour Cream* (p. 33), *Low-Fat Mayonnaise* (p. 32), or *Tofu Mayonnaise* (p. 31), puréed cooked or canned beans (or red lentils cooked 10 minutes), or a combination. Flavor simply with herbal salt or seasoned salt, or *Pesto* (p. 77) to taste. Or add ½ c. puréed roasted red peppers or reconstituted dried tomatoes (p. 46). Add some fresh garlic from a garlic press, maybe a chopped green onion or two (or some chives), and some chopped fresh herbs. Add a little more lemon juice if you like.

Or just add lots of fresh herbs, like dill and basil, with a little more salt and lemon juice to taste.

For a Mexican-style dip, just add your favorite hot tomato salsa to taste, and serve with baked tortilla chips.

chips and dippers

Besides raw vegetable dippers (crudités), there are now some wonderful baked tortilla and potato chips available from natural food stores and some super-markets. They have little or no fat. From your super-market you can buy pita crisps and bagel chips, melba toast, rye crisp bread, fat-free crackers, brown rice wafers, rice cakes, baked pretzels, and bread sticks (crispini). Check the ingredients and fat content on the labels before buying—these may vary from brand to brand.

bruschetta

You can make your own very inexpensive (and trendy) bruschetta to go with spreads and pâtés. Choose the best, rustic-style Italian or French bread you can find—a chewy bread with a porous texture and a crackly crust. Sourdough is good. Cut the bread into slices ½"-¾" thick. The traditional way to prepare the bread is to grill it or broil it in your oven 4"-6" from the heat, one side at a time, but you can cheat and use a toaster or toaster oven!

When golden and crunchy, serve the bruschetta plain with *White Bean Pâté* (p. 52), *Hummus With a Kick* (p. 51), *Tofu-Miso Pâté* (p. 49), *Pesto* (p. 77), or any other favorite low-fat spread. Rub each slice with a peeled garlic clove first, if you like.

The traditional Italian topping is diced, fresh, ripe tomatoes seasoned with salt and pepper and plenty of fresh basil and garlic—a sort of Italian "salsa." Or use bottled, commercial, vegetarian antipasto relish. Garlic-flavored, chopped, steam-fried leafy greens, or mushrooms are also delicious toppings.

tofu shakes

Serves 2

1 frozen banana (peeled before freezing), cut into chunks

1 c. orange or other fruit juice

½ (10.5 oz.) box reduced-fat, firm SILKEN tofu, or ½ c. (4 oz.) reduced-fat, medium-firm tofu

OPTIONAL: a handful of berries, or other fresh or frozen fruit

OPTIONAL: ½ tsp. dairy-free acidophilus powder

per serving: calories: 139, protein: 6 gm., fat: 1 gm., carbohydrates: 26 gm.

Satisfying any time of the day! The mixture can also be frozen in popsicle molds.

Combine everything in the blender until smooth. Pour into 2 glasses and drink immediately.

orange or pineapple "julia"

Serves 2
(can be soy-free)

¾ c. water

6 T. frozen orange juice or pineapple juice concentrate

⅓ c. reduced-fat, firm SILKEN tofu, or ¼ c. reduced-fat, firm or medium-firm tofu

½ tsp. vanilla extract

5 ice cubes

per serving: calories: 87, protein: 4 gm., fat: 0 gm., carbohydrates: 17 gm.

This makes a great snack, breakfast, or dessert.

Mix everything but the ice cubes in the blender until smooth. Add the ice cubes and blend again. Pour into 2 glasses and serve.

To Make Soy-Free: Omit the tofu and water, and use 1 c. soy-free non-dairy milk.

chocolate "milk" shakes

Serves 2
(can be soy-free)

1 c. reduced-fat, non-dairy milk
½ c. reduced-fat, medium-firm tofu, or
½ (10.5 oz.) box reduced-fat, firm
SILKEN tofu
¼ c. reduced-fat tofu beverage mix
powder or other good-tasting non-
dairy "milk" powder (NOT
unflavored soymilk powder)
¼ c. Sucanat or sugar
2 T. unsweetened cocoa powder
1 tsp. vanilla extract, or ½ tsp.
peppermint extract
10 ice cubes

per serving: calories: 240, protein: 16 gm.,
fat: 3 gm., carbohydrates: 39 gm.

Your children will love you for this!

Mix everything except the ice cubes in a blender until smooth. Add the ice cubes 2 at a time, blending briefly after each addition. When all the ice cubes are added, blend until the mixture is smooth and thick. Pour into 2 glasses and serve immediately.

To Make Soy-Free: Omit the tofu and use 1 banana, cut into chunks.

Strawberry "Milk" Shakes: Omit the cocoa, use white or turbinado sugar, and add ½ c. sliced fresh or frozen strawberries. Use only ½ tsp. vanilla extract.
Vanilla "Milk" Shakes: Omit the cocoa, use white or turbinado sugar, and increase the vanilla to 2 tsp.

lassi

(indian "yogurt" and fruit shake)

Serves 3 to 4
(can be soy-free)

½ c. apricot nectar, frozen papaya, or
 pineapple juice concentrate, or
 ⅔ c. chopped, ripe, peeled mango,
 papaya, pineapple, or canned,
 unsweetened pineapple
1 c. cold water
⅓ c. frozen apple juice concentrate, or
 ¼ c. liquid sweetener
½ (10.5 oz.) box reduced-fat, firm SILKEN
 tofu, or ½ c. reduced-fat, medium-
 firm tofu or commercial soy yogurt
6 ice cubes
2 T. lemon or lime juice
¼ tsp. coconut extract or ground
 cardamom, nutmeg, or ginger
OPTIONAL: 1 tsp. dairy-free acidophilus
 powder

A refreshing dessert, snack, or breakfast beverage with tropical overtones.

Place all the ingredients, except the ice cubes, in the blender, and blend until smooth. Add the ice cubes and blend again until the ice is finely ground. Pour into 3 or 4 glasses, and serve immediately.

To Make Soy-Free: Omit the tofu and use 1½ c. soy-free, non-dairy milk instead of water.

per serving: calories: 84, protein: 3 gm., fat: 1 gm., carbohydrates: 26 gm.

quick hot cocoa mix

Makes enough mix for 8 cups cocoa
(can be soy-free)

1½ c. reduced-fat tofu beverage mix or other good-tasting, low-fat, non-dairy "milk" powder (NOT unflavored soymilk powder)
⅓-½ c. unsweetened cocoa (depending on how much chocolate you like)
½ c. Sucanat or sugar
½ tsp. salt

per cup: calories: 149, protein: 14 gm., fat: 0 gm., carbohydrates: 21 gm.

If hot cocoa is your "comfort food," keep this mix around at all times. Or give it to vegan friends for gifts.

Mix the ingredients well with a whisk in a medium bowl. Store in an airtight container.

For each cup of cocoa, combine a scant ⅓ c. of the cocoa mix with 1 c. boiling water and ¼ tsp. vanilla extract, or ⅛ tsp. almond or peppermint extract in a blender until well blended and smooth. (Take the plastic center part of the blender lid out, and cover the hole in the top with a folded tea towel before blending. This prevents steam build-up inside the blender, which can cause hot liquid to explode out.) Pour into a mug and serve immediately.

Microwave Option: Blend the mixture using cold non-dairy milk. Pour into a large microwave-safe mug, and microwave on high for 1½ minutes. Whisk before serving.

Variations:
1. For Mexican chocolate, add a pinch of cinnamon.
2. For Christmas breakfast, use a candy-cane stir-stick.
3. For a mocha version, add 1 tsp. instant coffee or coffee substitute.
4. For Norwegian chocolate, add 1 tsp. rum (or a few drops of rum extract) and a drop of butter flavoring extract.
5. For a *special* cocoa, add a tablespoon or so of chocolate, coffee, orange, almond, or other favorite liqueur, brandy, or rum to the cocoa.

speedy soups, sauces & salads

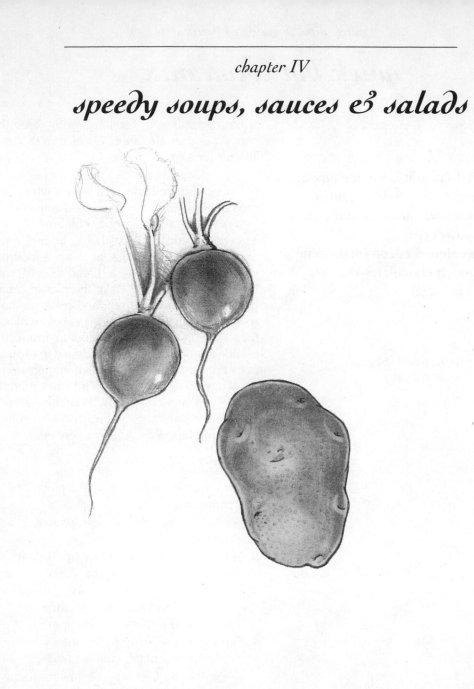

soups

It may seem odd to have so many soup recipes in a book on quick cooking, since canned and packaged soups abound on supermarket shelves. But how many of those soups are vegan or even vegetarian? And how many are as hearty as the television ads would have you believe?

I was fortunate to have grown up with a mother who made real soup, and I still think that a good homemade soup is one of the best meals going—any time of the day. You can come home from work and throw together a fine pot of soup in 10 minutes. Ten or fifteen minutes more of simmering (while you make a sandwich, slice some crusty bread or heat rolls, or make a salad) and the family can sit down to a comforting, nutritious meal not to be found in any fast food restaurant. Double the recipe and you can freeze leftovers to reheat for another meal.

I had a great time working on this section, conjuring up memories of favorite soups from non-vegetarian days and then heading into the kitchen to devise quick AND vegetarian versions of them (the Manhattan and New England-style chowders, sans clams, are two examples). I hope you enjoy the results!

converting high-fat, non-vegan soup recipes

Steam-fry instead of sauté; use vegetarian broth or bean broth for stock; use ½ c. tofu, mashed potatoes, or canned white beans blended with ½ c. water, or use *plain rice milk*, in place of cream or evaporated milk. (A tablespoon or 2 of raw cashews, at 3 gm. fat each, can be added if you want extra richness without soy.) Use soy bacon chips if the recipe calls for bacon.

basic quick soup ingredients

Keep your favorite vegetarian broth cubes or powder, canned beans, and diced tomatoes, and frozen and long-keeping staple vegetables around for spur-of-the-moment pots of goodness. For practically instant soups, instant mashed potatoes, dried onion flakes, split red lentils, vegetable flakes, bean flakes (pinto and black), and bean flours are handy. You can also improvise with with such ingredients as canned pumpkin in a creamy squash soup.

leftovers into soup

Leftovers can make delicious soups. For instance, you can thin out leftover mashed potatoes with non-dairy milk and broth, add seasonings, and have instant creamy potato soup! Add frozen spinach and it's a whole new dish. I once made a delicious soup out of the leftovers from a whole meal—black beans, brown rice, sweet potatoes, and kale all went into the pot with some broth.

meat-free soup flavorings

For the taste of smoked meats that we associate with many soups, experiment with soy bacon bits or chips, bits of vegetarian "back bacon," "ham," or "pepperoni," smoked tofu or *Smoky Pan-Fried Tofu* (p. 30), liquid smoke, or sliced tofu wieners.

Taste-test all of the "chicken-like" vegetarian cubes and powders you can find in your area—there are some excellent ones. Vegetarian broth can be made even more "chicken-like" with the addition of a little nutritional yeast and soy sauce.

Vegetarian broth can be "beefed-up" with the addition of a little yeast extract (like Marmite), reduced broth from soaking dried mushrooms, dark red miso, or lite (low-sodium) soy sauce.

cheezy corn and frank chowder

Serves 6
(can be soy-free)

1 large onion, chopped
4 cloves garlic, minced
1 c. sliced celery
1 lb. (4 medium) waxy potatoes, peeled (or scrubbed unpeeled) and diced
4 c. vegetarian broth
1 c. frozen corn kernels
1 lb. reduced-fat, medium-firm tofu
1 T. lemon juice
1 T. cornstarch
4 low-fat tofu wieners, sliced thinly into "coins"
¼ c. nutritional yeast flakes
¼ c. minced fresh parsley
2 tsp. dry mustard
1 tsp. salt, or 1 T. light miso plus ½ tsp. salt
¼ tsp. black or white pepper

per serving: calories: 251, protein: 18 gm.,
fat: 5 gm., carbohydrates: 34 gm.

This chowder is thick and rich-tasting whichever way you make it!

In a medium pot, steam-fry the onion, garlic, and celery until they begin to soften, about 5 minutes. Add the broth, potatoes, and corn. Simmer about 10 minutes or until the potatoes are soft. Add the wiener slices, yeast, parsley, mustard, salt, and pepper. Purée the tofu in a blender with some of the broth from the pot, the cornstarch, and lemon juice until VERY smooth. Pour this into the pot, and stir over medium-high heat until it thickens. Serve immediately.

To Make Soy-Free: Omit the tofu wieners and tofu. For liquid, use 2 c. vegetarian broth and 2 c. soy-free non-dairy "milk," plus 2 heaping tsp. vegetarian broth powder (soy-free). Replace the tofu in the blended mixture with 1 c. cooked short grain rice. If you use the miso, use chick-pea miso.

Variations:
1. Add some chopped red and/or green bell pepper and/or a chopped, peeled carrot along with the potatoes.
2. Omit the tofu wieners and use low-fat vegetarian "sausage," 1 T. soy bacon chips, or about ¼ c. chopped vegetarian "ham" or "back bacon."
3. Omit the wieners and use 2 c. corn. Add an 8 oz. can of chopped green chiles and 1 chopped, canned jalapeño chile, or 2 tsp. chopped chiles chipotles in adobado sauce, plus ½ tsp. ground cumin.

savory white bean and corn soup

Serves 6
(soy-free)

1 large onion, minced
2 cloves garlic, minced
2 (15 oz.) cans white kidney, cannellini,
    Great Northern, or navy beans,
    drained (3 c. cooked)
2 c. vegetarian broth
1 (14 oz.) can diced tomatoes and juice
1 (8 oz.) can cream-style corn (about
    1 c.)
1 tsp. dried savory
½-1 tsp. salt
freshly ground black pepper, to taste

per serving: calories: 178, protein: 8 gm.,
fat: 0 gm., carbohydrates: 35 gm.

This is great with focaccia or a wedge of left-over pizza.

In a medium pot, steam-fry the onion and garlic for about 5 minutes, or until it begins to soften. Add the beans and broth, and mash the beans coarsely with a potato masher. Add the remaining ingredients and simmer for 10 minutes. Taste for seasoning and serve.

new england-style sea vegetable chowder

Serves 4-6
(can be soy-free)

1 large onion, chopped
4 medium waxy potatoes (1 lb.), peeled
  and diced
2 c. vegetarian broth
1-2 c. chopped oyster mushrooms, or
  ½ c. dry textured vegetable
  protein granules and 7 T. water
1 c. frozen corn kernels
½ c. crumbled dry dulse, or ¼ c. dulse
  flakes
¼ c. minced fresh parsley
1 bay leaf
1 T. soy bacon chips (omit for soy-free)
½ tsp. dried thyme
¼ tsp. kelp powder
freshly ground black pepper, to taste
paprika

BLENDED MIXTURE
1 (10.5 oz.) box reduced-fat, extra-firm
  SILKEN tofu, or 1 c. reduced-fat,
  medium-firm tofu
1 c. water
2 tsp. salt
1 tsp. sugar or alternate

Dulse is a sea vegetable which is gathered on the northeastern coast of North America, so I thought it would be an appropriate substitute for a clam flavor, along with oyster mushrooms or textured vegetable protein granules. This soup rivals calorie-rich and fat-laden versions for flavor and texture.

In a medium pot, steam-fry the onions for about 5 minutes, or until softened. Add all the ingredients except the pepper, paprika, and Blended Mixture. Cover and simmer for about 10 minutes, or until the potatoes are soft.

Meanwhile, whip the Blended Mixture ingredients in a blender until VERY smooth. When the potatoes are soft, stir in the Blended Mixture, add pepper to taste, and heat gently. Sprinkle each serving with paprika. Serve with crackers.

To Make Soy-Free: Use mushrooms and soy-free broth. In the Blended Mixture, omit the tofu and use 1 c. cooked short grain rice and ¼ c. raw cashews (this adds about 2 gm. of fat per serving).

per serving: calories: 182, protein: 11 gm., fat: 1 gm., carbohydrates: 32 gm.

manhattan-style chowder

Serves 6
(can be soy-free)

1 large onion, peeled and cut in chunks
1 large carrot, peeled and cut in chunks
2 large cloves garlic, peeled
½ large green pepper, seeded and diced
3 c. vegetarian broth
1 (28 oz.) can diced tomatoes
**2 medium waxy potatoes, peeled and
    diced**
1 c. sliced celery
**1 c. chopped oyster mushrooms, or ½ c.
    dry textured vegetable protein
    granules and ⅓ c. water**
**½ c. dry crumbled dulse, or ¼ c. dulse
    flakes**
¼ c. minced fresh parsley
1 tsp. salt
1 bay leaf
½ tsp. dried thyme
½ tsp. kelp powder
**pinch cayenne pepper and freshly
    ground black pepper**
OPTIONAL: **1 c. frozen corn kernels**
½ c. dry white wine or white vermouth
1 T. soy bacon bits or chips

For devotees of the tomato-flavored version, a spicy, vegetable-thick chowder.

Mince the onion, carrot, and garlic in the food processor. In a medium pot, steam-fry the minced vegetables for about 5 minutes, or until softened. Add all the ingredients, bring to a boil, then reduce heat, cover, and simmer for 15 minutes.

per serving: calories: 103, protein: 5 gm.,
fat: 0 gm., carbohydrates: 20 gm.

creamy vegetable soup

Serves 4
(soy-free)

1 medium onion, chopped
1 clove garlic, minced
OPTIONAL: **2 stalks celery, chopped**
1 lb. vegetables of choice, chopped (see
possibilities below right)
2 medium russet potatoes (½ lb.),
peeled and diced
3 c. vegetarian broth
½ tsp. salt
pepper, to taste
OPTIONAL: **(any or all)**
1-3 tsp. lemon juice
1 T. curry powder
2 tsp. powdered ginger
¼ tsp. nutmeg
pinch cayenne
for garnish: plain soy yogurt or *Soy-Free*
Sour Cream* (p. 33), *Tofu Sour
Cream* (p. 35), or *Tofu-Cashew Sour
***Cream* (p. 36)**
minced fresh parsley, mint, basil, or
cilantro
paprika
curry powder
croutons
dillweed
chopped green onions or chives

A very simple concept—you simmer potatoes and whatever vegetable you like in broth, then purée it for a thick and creamy soup without fat, dairy, nuts, or even soy. This soup can be served hot or cold.

ALLERGY NOTE: If you can't eat potatoes, substitute about 2 c. of drained cooked or canned white beans, or cooked short grain rice.

In a medium pot, steam-fry the onion and garlic for 5 minutes. Add the vegetables, potatoes, broth, salt, and optional seasonings (except lemon juice). Bring to a boil, cover, turn down, and simmer about 10-15 minutes, or until the vegetables and potatoes are tender. Purée right in the pot with a hand blender, or, with a slotted spoon, transfer all the solids to a food processor, and purée until smooth. Add a bit of the broth, then stir the puréed mixture back into the pot. Taste for salt and pepper. Add lemon juice, if using.

Serve with one or two garnishes.

Vegetable Possibilities:
carrots
zucchini or other summer squash
pumpkin (14 oz. can), acorn, butternut, or
other winter squash, or sweet potato
(perhaps with an apple added)
leafy greens (10 oz. chopped frozen)
cauliflower
broccoli
asparagus
leeks

per serving: calories: 98, protein: 3 gm.,
fat: 0 gm., carbohydrates: 22 gm.

vegetarian caldo verde
(portuguese kale and potato soup)

Serves 6-8
(soy-free)

1 large onion, peeled and cut in chunks
2 whole heads of garlic, peeled, or
   ¼-½ c. prepared minced garlic
1 bay leaf
1 tsp. paprika
1 tsp. ground cumin
½ tsp. dried red chile flakes, or a pinch
   of cayenne
6 c. vegetarian broth
½ lb. kale or turnip greens, washed and
   chopped small, or 1 (10 oz.) pkg.
   frozen greens, thawed, squeezed
   dry, and chopped
4 medium red-skinned potatoes (1 lb.),
   thinly sliced
¼ c. dry red wine, or 1 T. balsamic
   vinegar
salt and pepper to taste
OPTIONAL: **1 (15 oz.) can red beans**
   (1½ c. cooked), or 2 or 3 low-fat
   tofu wieners, sausages, or spicy
   links, sliced into "coins"

Kale and potatoes are made for each other, as you'll see when you try this wonderful soup. In Portugal, it is usually made with a spicy sausage called chorizo, which is seasoned with garlic, dry red wine, chile, paprika, and cumin. I add these flavorings to the soup instead.

NOTE: Don't be concerned about the amount of garlic called for—it mellows with cooking.

Mince the onion and garlic in a food processor. Steam-fry these in a medium pot for 5 minutes, or until softened. Add the bay leaf, paprika, cumin, and chile, and stir for 1 minute.

Add the remaining ingredients, bring to a boil, cover, and lower the heat. Simmer for 15 minutes. Add salt and pepper to taste.

per serving: calories: 100, protein: 2 gm.,
fat: 0 gm., carbohydrates: 20 gm.

choose-your-own-vegetables quick minestrone

Serves 4-6
(soy-free)

1 large onion, chopped
4 large cloves garlic, minced
2 stalks celery, chopped
1 (28 oz.) can diced tomatoes and juice
4 c. vegetarian broth
2-3 c. chopped vegetables, such as:
   bell pepper
   broccoli
   cabbage
   carrots
   cauliflower
   eggplant
   green beans, small whole, frozen
   kale and other greens
   potatoes
   spinach (fresh or frozen)
   zucchini
1 (15 oz.) can plain beans of your
   choice, drained (1½ c. cooked)
1 c. macaroni, small shell pasta, or
   broken spaghetti
a handful of fresh minced parsley
½ tsp. dry basil
salt and pepper, to taste
OPTIONAL: **soy Parmesan**

I often used to make this soup from leftovers when I had a house full of hungry children. It's also delicious when you start with canned beans.

In a medium pot, steam-fry the onion, garlic, and celery for about 5 minutes. Add the remaining ingredients, except the salt, pepper, and soy parmesan, if using. Bring to a boil, then turn down, cover, and simmer for 15-20 minutes. Taste for salt and pepper. If it's too thick for your liking, add more broth. Serve hot with soy parmesan to sprinkle on top, if you wish.

per serving: calories: 241, protein: 9 gm.,
fat: 0 gm., carbohydrates: 50 gm.

food processor gazpacho with black beans

Serves 4-6
(soy-free)

½ medium cucumber (peel if necessary),
 cut in chunks
1 medium ripe, firm tomato, trimmed
 and cut in chunks
1 small onion, cut in chunks
½ large green pepper, seeded and cut in
 chunks
1 clove garlic, peeled
3 c. chilled tomato juice or vegetable
 cocktail
1½ c. cooked black beans, or 1 (15 oz.)
 can, drained
2 T. red wine vinegar or balsamic
 vinegar
1 T. fresh parsley or basil
½ tsp. sugar or alternate
OPTIONAL: ½ tsp. *Vegetarian
 Worcestershire Sauce* (p. 77)
½ tsp. salt
croutons

The addition of canned black beans adds color contrast and makes a meal out of this cold summer soup.

Mince the cucumber, onion, tomato, green pepper, and garlic in the food processor. Pour into a serving bowl with all the other ingredients, except the croutons. Mix well and serve immediately, or chill. Serve with croutons to sprinkle on top.

per serving: calories: 118, protein: 5 gm.,
fat: 0 gm., carbohydrates: 23 gm.

super-quick chickenless noodle soup

Serves 6-8
(can be soy-free)

10 c. chicken-style vegetarian broth
1-2 c. broken cappellini or vermicelli
pasta (very thin spaghetti), or
Oriental rice vermicelli (4-7 oz.)
½ c. dried soup vegetable flakes
½ c. dry textured vegetable protein
granules, or ¾-1 c. crumbled,
thawed frozen tofu or chopped
mushrooms
¼ c. nutritional yeast flakes
¼ c. minced fresh parsley
2 T. lite soy sauce (or alternate, p. 13)
2 T. dried onion flakes
1 tsp. garlic granules
½ tsp. white pepper
OPTIONAL: **1 c. frozen petit pois (baby**
peas)

per serving: calories: 58, protein: 6 gm., fat: 0 gm.,
carbohydrates: 8 gm.

Many of us grew up on canned, packaged, or even homemade chicken noodle soup, and it remains one of the number one "comfort foods" in North America. Fortunately, it's easy to make without sacrificing any chickens!

Place everything in a large pot, and bring to a boil. Turn down the heat, cover, and simmer for about 10 minutes. Serve with crackers or toast.

When you have a cold: Add about ¼ tsp. cayenne pepper, and omit the garlic granules, squeezing a whole fresh clove of garlic from a garlic press directly into each bowl of soup.

chinese hot and sour soup

Serves 4-6
(can be soy-free)

4 c. vegetarian broth

6 oz. reduced-fat, medium-firm tofu, or seitan or mushrooms

4 oz. sauerkraut

½ c. frozen peas (preferably petit pois)

½ c. sliced, fresh mushrooms (button, shiitake, or oyster)

3 dried Chinese mushrooms, ground to a powder in a DRY blender

2 green onions, chopped

2 slices fresh gingerroot, chopped

2 T. dry sherry

1-2 T. soy sauce (or alternate, p. 13)

1 T. rice vinegar, cider vinegar, or white wine vinegar (or more to taste)

½ tsp. liquid hot pepper seasoning (or more to taste)

1 T. cornstarch dissolved in 1 T. cold water

OPTIONAL:

a sprinkling of ground Szechuan pepper

julienne strips of carrot or other vegetable

a sprinkling of Chinese roasted sesame oil

This popular soup is easy to make at home, and it's great for cold-sufferers! The sauerkraut is a similar and more easily obtainable substitute for Szechuan preserved vegetables.

In a medium pot, place all of the ingredients except the dissolved cornstarch and the optional ingredients. Bring to a boil, then turn down and simmer for about 5-10 minutes. Add the dissolved cornstarch and optional ingredients. Bring to a boil, stirring until it has thickened slightly and is clear. Serve immediately.

per serving: calories: 76, protein: 5 gm., fat: 2 gm., carbohydrates: 8 gm.

sauces

Here is a small collection of basic sauces which can be used to enhance your meals in many ways. When you're in a hurry, you'll probably prefer to use your favorite commercial brand of meatless spaghetti sauce (marinara sauce), but I think you'll find the recipe in this chapter superior in taste and much lower in cost. You can make it up in quantity when you have time, and freeze it.

Barbecue sauce is another item that you will likely buy rather than make most of the time, but give our delicious and easy *Red Chile and Orange Barbecue Sauce* a try. It keeps in the refrigerator for weeks and can be used to coat grilled or broiled extra-firm tofu, textured soy protein chunks, seitan, or vegetables for quick gourmet meals.

The other sauces (and one gravy) are ones that you may have trouble finding in low-fat, meat-and-dairy-free versions. They take only minutes to make and are so versatile that no leftovers will go to waste!

creamy tomato sauce

Makes 3 cups
(can be soy-free)

1⅓ c. water
1 (6 oz.) can good quality tomato paste
1 c. reduced-fat soymilk or other non-dairy milk
¼ c. dry white wine (can be non-alcoholic)
½ tsp. salt
½ tsp. dried thyme
¼ tsp. black pepper

This is one of the easiest homemade sauces you'll ever make. Use it on pasta of all kinds (stuffed ones, like ravioli, in particular), frozen potato and onion pyrogies, savory crepes, cauliflower, etc.

Whisk or blend all of the ingredients together until smooth. Pour into a small, heavy saucepan, and bring to a boil over medium heat, stirring now and then. Turn the heat to low, and simmer gently for a few minutes. Remove from the heat.

per ½ cup: calories: 51, protein: 1 gm., fat: 0 gm., carbohydrates: 8 gm.

red chile and orange barbecue sauce

makes about 3½ cups
(can be soy-free)

1¾ c. ketchup (fruit-sweetened, if you like)
1 c. orange juice (preferably freshly squeezed)
⅓ c. water
¼ c. fancy molasses
¼ c. lemon juice (preferably freshly squeezed)
3 T. chile powder
2 T. soy sauce (or alternate, p. 13)
2 T. *Vegetarian Worcestershire Sauce* (p. 77)
1 T. dry mustard
2 tsp. onion powder

2 bay leaves
1½ tsp. dried oregano
1½ tsp. powdered ginger
1 tsp. curry powder
1 tsp. pepper
1 tsp. dried red chile flakes
½ tsp. garlic granules

Even if you usually buy barbecue sauce, you might like to give this delicious homemade one a try. It will keep for weeks in a jar in the refrigerator.

Mix all of the ingredients in a heavy-bottomed medium pot, bring to a boil, then simmer on low, uncovered, for 15 to 20 minutes.

per ½ cup: calories: 125, protein: 2 gm., fat: 0 gm., carbohydrates: 28 gm.

golden cheeze sauce or rarebit

Serves 6
(soy-free)

1 recipe *Melty Chedda' Cheeze* (p. 43)
1-1¼ c. non-dairy milk, beer, or dry
white wine (can be non-alcoholic)
salt to taste
OPTIONAL: **(any or all)**
pinch of nutmeg
pinch of white pepper
soy bacon chips

per ½ cup: calories: 64, protein: 15 gm.,
fat: 1 gm., carbohydrates: 8 gm.

This is used like a rich cheddar cheese sauce on steamed vegetables (especially cauliflower), macaroni, on top of casseroles or nachos. You can also add it to leftover soups.

Make the Melty Chedda' Cheeze, whisk in the milk to make a sauce, and add any seasonings. Heat briefly in a microwave or on top of the stove. If you are using cold, leftover cheeze, blend it up with an equal amount of non-dairy milk until smooth, and then heat.

Variation: You can also use *Melty Pizza Cheeze* (p. 42) or *Melty Jack Cheeze* (p. 43) instead of the the *Melty Chedda' Cheeze* to make a white sauce. Use dry white wine (can be non-alcoholic) with the *Melty Suisse Cheeze* (p. 43) for fondue.

For a nacho sauce, add some drained black beans, chopped jalapeños or other chiles, chopped olives, and a pinch of cumin to the sauces made with either *Melty Chedda' Cheeze* or *Melty Jack Cheeze*.

rich brown yeast gravy

Makes about 2½ cups
(can be soy-free)

⅓ c. unbleached all-purpose or whole wheat pastry flour

⅓ cup nutritional yeast flakes

2½ c. water

2 T. soy sauce or mushroom soy sauce (or alternate, p. 13)

½ tsp. salt

OPTIONAL:

a few shakes of gravy browner, if the gravy seems too light in color

fresh or dried chopped herbs

steam-fried mushrooms

steam-fried onions

crumbled *Vegetarian "Sausage"* (p. 28) ground seitan

crushed fresh garlic, or ¼ tsp. garlic granules.

per ¼ cup: calories: 28, protein: 2 gm., fat: 0 gm., carbohydrates: 5 gm.

There are many variations of this recipe, but this is my standard, fat-free take on it, and very popular it is! It's excellent on potatoes, rice, tofu, seitan, biscuits, and much, much more.

Whisk the flour and nutritional yeast in a heavy saucepan over high heat. When it smells toasty, remove from the heat and whisk in the rest of the ingredients, or mix in a blender to avoid lumps.

Place over high heat again, and stir until it thickens and comes to a boil. Reduce the heat and cook for 2-5 minutes.

This keeps well in the refrigerator for a week. It will thicken up when chilled, so you'll probably have to add a bit of water when reheating. For variety, substitute dry white or red wine or mushroom cooking or soaking liquid for half the water. For a giblet-style gravy, add 1 cup chopped seitan or prepared textured vegetable protein chunks.

Microwave Option: In a 1½ qt. microwave-proof bowl, mix the flour and yeast. Toast this in the microwave on high for 3 minutes, uncovered. Whisk in the remaining ingredients. Cover and cook on high 3 minutes; whisk. Cover and cook again for 3 minutes on high; whisk. Or, make ½ the recipe in a 4 c. microwave-safe glass measuring container, and cook as above, but in 2 minute increments.

on-the-spot creamy "butter" sauce
("hollandaise")

Makes 1¼ cups
(can be soy-free)

1 c. water
⅓ c. reduced-fat, medium-firm tofu
1 T. EACH cornstarch and lemon juice
2 tsp. good-tasting, non-dairy "milk"
    powder
1-2 tsp. dried herbs of choice, or
    1-2 T. minced fresh herbs
1½ tsp. nutritional yeast
1 tsp. salt
½ tsp. onion powder
⅛-¼ tsp. garlic granules, or 1 small
    clove garlic, peeled
⅛ tsp. EACH paprika and turmeric

per ¼ cup: calories: 28, protein: 3 gm., fat: 1 gm.,
carbohydrates: 3 gm.

This is the perfect sauce for veggies. You can whip this up while they're steaming.

Combine everything until smooth in a blender or food processor. Either cook it in a small saucepan over high heat, stirring constantly, until it has thickened.

Microwave Option: Microwave it in a 4 c. glass measuring beaker or microwave-safe bowl for 2 minutes; whisk. Then microwave 2 minutes more; whisk. Serve hot.

Refrigerate leftovers in a covered jar, and reheat by microwaving for a minute or two, or stirring over medium heat in a saucepan until hot.

To Make Soy-Free: Omit the tofu and "milk" powder, and reduce the cornstarch to 2 tsp. Add ¼ c. raw cashews. This will add 1.5 gm. of fat per 2 T.

quick creamy sauce

Makes about 4½ cups (enough for about 2 lbs. pasta or 6 servings)
(can be soy-free)

1½ c. cold water
1 (10.5 oz.) box reduced-fat, extra-firm SILKEN tofu, or ½ lb. reduced-fat, medium-firm or firm tofu
¼ c. dry white wine, or 3 T. water and 1 T. balsamic vinegar or lemon juice
⅓ c. nutritional yeast flakes
2 T. cornstarch
1½ T. chicken-style broth powder
2 tsp. salt, or 2 T. light miso and 1 tsp. salt
2 tsp. garlic granules
1½ c. hot or boiling water

per serving: calories: 63, protein: 6 gm., fat: 1 gm., carbohydrates: 6 gm.

This is one of the most versatile and effortless sauces around, so don't be afraid to make this large amount. It can be used in a number of pasta dishes (see Chapter. V). Leftovers can be used in creamy soups and casseroles, to moisten stuffed baked potatoes or mashed potatoes, and on vegetables.

Combine all of the ingredients, except the hot water, and blend until smooth. Add the water and blend again. Pour the mixture into a heavy saucepan, and stir over high heat constantly until it comes to a boil. Turn down the heat and simmer on low for a few minutes.

Microwave Option: Pour the blended mixture into a large, microwave-safe bowl. Cover and cook on high for 3 minutes. Whisk well, cover, and cook on high for 3 more minutes, or until thickened. Whisk well.

To Make Soy-Free: Omit all 3 c. water and the tofu, and replace with 1 qt. soy-free nondairy "milk." Use 3½ T. cornstarch instead of 2 T. Replace the soy miso with chick-pea miso.

quick marinara sauce

Makes 6-8 cups
(soy-free)

2 c. minced onions
2-4 cloves garlic, minced
1 (28 oz.) can whole tomatoes and their juice
1 (6 oz.) can tomato paste
1 tsp. dried basil
1 tsp. dried oregano
1 bay leaf
½ tsp. sweetener of your choice
salt and pepper, to taste
OPTIONAL:
   fresh mushrooms, chopped or sliced
   carrot, minced or grated
   green pepper, chopped
   fresh parsley and/or other fresh herbs, chopped
   dried rosemary, marjoram, and or sage
   hot red pepper flakes

per cup: calories: 58, protein: 2 gm., fat: 0 gm., carbohydrates: 12 gm.

This will probably be part of a staple meal for many people, because spaghetti and tomato sauce is a satisfying dish. Vary it by using a different kind of pasta each time—rotelle, rigatoni, penne, linguine, etc.

In a large, heavy, lightly oiled or nonstick pot, steam-fry the onions, garlic, and any of the optional ingredients until the onions are soft.

If you have time, you may want to add the tomato paste to the softened onions and garlic, and stir constantly over medium heat until the paste begins to darken. This is a method used by many Italian cooks to add flavor to tomato sauces made with paste, by caramelizing the natural tomato sugars. If you choose not to do this, just add the tomato paste along with the tomatoes.

Add the tomatoes and juice, tomato paste (if not already used), basil, oregano, bay leaf, sweetener, salt, and pepper. Crush the tomatoes with your fingers or the back of a large spoon as you pour them in to the pot. If the mixture is too thick, add some water or dry red wine. Bring to a boil, reduce the heat to low, cover, and simmer for about 15 minutes. Taste and adjust the seasonings.

"you won't believe it" pesto

Makes 1½ cups
(can be soy-free)

4 c. fresh basil leaves (loosely-packed)
8 cloves garlic, peeled
6 oz. (¾ c.) reduced-fat, firm or medium-firm tofu, or ½ (10.5 oz.) box reduced-fat, extra-firm SILKEN tofu
¼ c. nutritional yeast flakes
1½ T. chicken-like broth powder
1 T. lemon juice
1½ tsp. salt (use less if your broth powder is salty)

per 2 tablespoons: calories: 50, protein: 4 gm., fat: 1 gm., carbohydrates: 6 gm.

This pesto contains no cheese, no nuts, and no oil! But it's scrumptious! It keeps in the refrigerator for a couple of weeks and also can be frozen (freeze it in ice cube trays or in mounds on a cookie sheet, then put the frozen cubes or mounds in a plastic bag in the freezer). Use it on pasta, Bruschetta (p. 53), or baked potatoes.

Place all the ingredients in a food processor, and process until a paste forms. Place in a tightly covered container (or freeze as directed above), and refrigerate until ready to use.

The top may darken a little, but this oxidation doesn't affect the taste or nutritive value—just stir the mixture before using.

To Make Soy-Free: Replace the tofu with ¾ c. well-drained, canned or cooked white beans or mashed potatoes, and check broth powder for soy products.

vegetarian worcestershire sauce

Makes 1½ cups
(can be soy-free)

1 c. cider vinegar
⅓ c. dark molasses
¼ c. soy sauce or mushroom sauce soy sauce (or alternate, p. 13)
¼ c. water
3 T. lemon juice
1½ tsp. salt
1½ tsp. mustard powder
1 tsp. onion powder
¾ tsp. ground ginger

½ tsp. black pepper
¼ tsp. garlic granules
¼ tsp. cayenne pepper
¼ tsp. ground cinnamon
⅛ tsp. ground cloves or allspice
⅛ tsp. ground cardamom

Combine all the ingredients in a blender. Pour into a saucepan and bring to a boil. Store in the refrigerator.

per tablespoon: calories: 10, protein: 0 gm., fat: 0 gm., carbohydrates: 3 gm.

salads and dressings

Although salads give scope for some of the greatest quick meals, I rarely follow recipes for them. I use what I have around, what's in season, and what sounds good to me. I'll give you a few recipes, but this section is basically dressings and ideas for making up your own full-meal salads.

I use a variety of homemade, oil-free dressings, but there are some acceptable commercial ones on the market now, so feel free to substitute your favorites for mine. If you prefer homemade dressings, you can use my *Oil Substitute for Salad Dressings* (p. 79), *Tofu Sour Cream* (p. 35), *Tofu Mayonnaise* (p. 31), or *Low-Fat Mayonnaise* (p. 32) in your own recipes (see index for soy-free versions). Feel free to change the proportions and seasonings in my recipes to suit your own taste; you may prefer a milder flavor than I do. Use some of those delicious gourmet herbal and fruit vinegars you might have received for gifts to give winter salads a lift. And don't forget to check out the *Flavored Mayonnaise* on p. 33.

Pair your salad creation with some good bread, and you have delightful eating in store!

for crisp lettuce

As soon as you pick the lettuce or bring it home, separate the leaves, discarding any bad ones, and soak in cold water for 15 minutes. Dry the leaves by using a salad spinner or laying them on a large, clean towel, rolling the towel up loosely, holding the ends firmly, and spinning the roll around. Remove the leaves, wrap them in moist towels, and place in a plastic bag (or in a special plastic salad storage container) in the refrigerator. Lettuce will keep fresh longer this way. This method can also be used for reviving wilted lettuce.

oil substitutes for salad dressings

Makes 1 cup
(soy-free)

1 cup cold water or light vegetarian broth
2 tsp. cornstarch

per tablespoon: calories: 1, protein: 0 gm., fat: 0 gm., carbohydrates: 0 gm.

Use this in place of the oil in your favorite dressings; it will thicken further when chilled.

Mix the ingredients in a small saucepan. Cook, stirring constantly, over high heat until thickened and clear.

If the dressing needs some thickening, use puréed fruit, puréed cooked beans or vegetables, a bit of blended silken or soft tofu, *Tofu Sour Cream* (p. 35), *Tofu Mayonnaise* (p. 31), *Low-Fat Mayonnaise* (p. 32), or commercial, low-fat mayonnaise. (See the Index for soy-free versions of any of these recipes.)

Variation: If you prefer, you can use cold white bean broth or garbanzo bean broth (the liquid the beans were cooked in) or potato cooking water for the cornstarch mixture. Other options might be tomato juice or vegetable juice cocktail, or other freshly extracted vegetable and fruit juices.

freezing bean broth

You can freeze bean broth in ice cube trays. Each one contains 2 T. Store the cubes in plastic bags in the freezer.

fruit and "cottage cheese" plate

Make the *Tofu "Cottage Cheese"* on p. 34. Mix it with some canned, unsweetened, crushed pineapple or pineapple tidbits. Mound each serving on a salad plate, and surround with fresh fruit (or a combination of canned and fresh). Decorate with fresh mint leaves.

coleslaw and carrot salad ideas

During the winter, the staple vegetables in our refrigerator are carrots and cabbages (of all kinds and colors!). I turn to these two old friends frequently for winter salads. Not only are they inexpensive and nutritious, but they are also deliciously crunchy when eaten raw.

You can grate them and eat either one alone with just a little dressing to moisten, or combine them. Chop them finely in the food processor if you are really in a hurry and don't mind a chopped, rather than shredded, texture. And/or add any other ingredients that strike your fancy:

chopped celery, jicama, sunchokes, or water chestnuts for more crunch

crispy apple chunks

raisins and other dried fruit

chopped or sliced onion, green onion, or chives

fresh herbs and parsley

grapes, bananas, orange sections, and other winter fruits

chunks of exotic fruits, such as mangoes

The *Easy Coleslaw Dressing* (p. 31) is the one I use most often on this type of salad, but try any favorite creamy or vinaigrette dressing. Oriental seasonings and vinegars also suit these vegetables (see *Thai Cabbage Salad* on p. 87).

For a presentation that lifts these salads from the ordinary to the sublime, place each serving of salad on a red cabbage leaf, and garnish with parsley or cilantro and citrus wedges.

chef's salad

This full-meal salad starts with a bed of crisp lettuce. I like to spread it out on a large platter or on individual dinner plates. Top artistically with several other ingredients, preferably with a variety of colors, textures, and nutritional components. Tomatoes, green onions, grated or pickled carrots, celery, red cabbage, well-rinsed, marinated artichoke hearts, raw or roasted peppers, arugula, fresh herbs, and other traditional salad ingredients can be used.

Then add a few of these suggestions:

croutons

strips of *Pan-Fried Breast of Tofu* (p. 29) or *Smoky Pan-Fried Tofu* (p. 30)

Teriyaki Tofu Burgers (p. 108)

cooked, commercial marinated tofu or tempeh

strips of seitan

canned or marinated chick-peas or other beans

Four Bean Salad (p. 84) or commercial bean salad

homemade or commercial pickled vegetables

cold cooked vegetables, such as asparagus

Eggless Salad (p. 126)

Pan-Fried Breast of Tofu (p. 29), chopped and mixed with *Low-Fat Mayonnaise* (p. 32)

pasta or grain salad

Tofu "Cottage Cheese" (p. 34)

Marinated Tofu (p. 30)

Mock Tuna Salad (p. 127)

pickled or raw mushrooms

soy bacon chips

commercial vegetarian "deli meat" strips

strips of grilled brown mushrooms

I also like to add some sliced fruit, such as cantaloupe, orange slices, watermelon, fresh berries, or exotics like papaya.

Use any fat-free or low-fat dressing you prefer. Then stand back and accept the complements!

balsamic vinaigrette

Makes 1½ cups
(soy-free)

1 c. cold water or light vegetarian broth
2 tsp. cornstarch
½ c. balsamic vinegar
1-3 cloves garlic, crushed
1½ tsp. salt, or 2 tsp. herbal salt
OPTIONAL: **2 T. brown sugar or Sucanat**

per 2 tablespoons: calories: 5, protein: 0 gm.,
fat: 0 gm., carbohydrates: 1 gm.

*This is our favorite dressing, hands down! It
keeps for several weeks in the refrigerator—just
shake it a little before serving.*

Place the water or broth and cornstarch in a
small pot, and stir over high heat until it thickens, boils, and turns clear. Whisk or blend in
the remaining ingredients, bottle, and store in
the refrigerator.

Dijon-Balsamic Vinaigrette: Omit half the
salt and add 1½ T. Dijon mustard; a chopped
green onion is optional.
Roasted Garlic Balsamic Vinaigrette: Omit
the raw garlic and add instead a whole head
(10-12 cloves) of *Quick-Roasted Garlic* (p. 44).
Use only ⅓ c. balsamic vinegar and 1 tsp. salt;
add ¼ tsp. pepper and 1 T. Dijon mustard.
Combine all of the ingredients in a blender
until smooth and creamy. Delicious!
Creamy Balsamic Vinaigrette: Add ¼ c. *Tofu
Mayonnaise* (p. 31) or *Low-Fat Mayonnaise*
(p. 32).

creamy fresh herb dressing

Makes 3 cups
(can be soy-free)

12 oz. reduced-fat, medium-firm tofu
⅞ c. water
3-4 green onions, chopped
a handful of fresh herbs of choice,
  chopped (basil, tarragon, dill, etc.)
6 T. cider vinegar
2 cloves garlic, peeled
¾-1 tsp. salt
½ tsp. sugar or alternate

per 2 tablespoons: calories: 16, protein: 2 gm.,
fat: 1 gm., carbohydrates: 1 gm.

This dressing can add a touch of summer to winter salads and cole slaws.

Combine everything in a blender or food processor until VERY smooth. Bottle and refrigerate.

"Green Goddess" Dressing: Use tarragon and parsley for the fresh herbs. Add 1 T. light soy or chick-pea miso and an optional ½ tsp. kelp powder.

To Make Soy-Free: Omit the tofu, salt, and 2 T. of vinegar. Instead, use 1 recipe (2 c.) *Low-Fat Mayonnaise* (p. 32). You may need a little less water.

creamy "bacon"-orange dressing

Makes 1 cup
(can be soy-free)

6 T. freshly squeezed orange juice
  (from 1 large orange)
¼ c. EACH soft or medium-firm tofu AND
  low-fat or tofu mayonnaise (com-
  mercial, or see pps. 31-32)
1½ T. fresh lemon juice
1 T. Dijon mustard
white bulbs of 3 green onions, chopped
1 tsp. soy bacon bits or chips
1 tsp. sugar or Sucanat
1 large clove garlic, peeled

½ tsp. Chinese sesame oil
¼ tsp. salt

Place all the ingredients in a blender, and process until creamy. Refrigerate.

To Make Soy-Free: Use ½ c. commercial or homemade, soy-free, *Low-Fat Mayonnaise*, (p. 32), or *Soy-Free "Sour Cream"* (p. 33). Omit the soy "bacon" bits, and use 1 tsp. sesame oil and a drop of liquid smoke.

per 2 tablespoons: calories: 39, protein: 1 gm.,
fat: 2 gm., carbohydrates: 2 gm.

pasta primavera salad

(Pictured on the cover)

Serves 6-8
(can be soy-free)

SALAD

¾ lb. dry penne, rotelle, or fusilli (corkscrew) pasta

2 medium carrots, peeled and cut into thin oval slices, or 3 c. frozen sliced carrots

½ lb. frozen, whole, small green beans

1 large onion, chopped

1 (15 oz.) can red or white (cannellini) kidney beans, or chick-peas, drained (1½ c. cooked)

1 green bell pepper, seeded and diced

1 red bell pepper, seeded and diced

3 roma tomatoes, sliced

1 c. thinly sliced celery

2 T. white wine vinegar

1 tsp. salt

freshly ground black pepper, to taste

DRESSING

1 (10.5 oz.) box reduced-fat, firm or extra-firm SILKEN tofu

¼ c. lemon juice

¼ c. chopped fresh basil, or 1½ T. dried

1 T. white wine vinegar

1 tsp. salt

½ tsp. dry mustard powder

Here's a hearty full-meal salad that's good enough to serve to company. If you're allergic to wheat, use rice pasta.

Cook the pasta in a large pot of boiling, salted water. While it cooks, prepare the vegetables. When the pasta is almost half-cooked, add the raw carrots to the pot of simmering pasta. When the pasta is almost tender, add the green beans (and frozen carrot slices, if using). When the pasta is just tender, but still chewy, drain it with the carrots and green beans in a colander.

Place the drained pasta and vegetables in a large serving bowl with the onion, beans, peppers, tomatoes, and celery. Add the 2 T. vinegar, 1 tsp. salt, and pepper to taste. Toss well. Place the dressing ingredients in a blender or food processor, and blend until VERY smooth. Pour it over the warm pasta, and combine well. Cover and refrigerate until serving time. Serve at room temperature or cold.

To Make the Dressing Soy-Free: Omit the tofu, vinegar, salt, and mustard powder, and use 1⅓ c. *Low-Fat Mayonnaise* (p. 32), or use your favorite low-calorie vinaigrette.

per serving: calories: 159, protein: 9 gm., fat: 1 gm., carbohydrates: 29 gm.

four bean salad

Serves 6
(can be soy-free)

SALAD

1 (15 oz.) can chick-peas, drained (1½ c. cooked)

1 (15 oz.) can small red beans or red kidney beans, drained (1½ c. cooked)

1 (15 oz.) can black-eyed peas, drained (1½ c. cooked)

1 (15 oz.) can small, whole green beans, drained (1½ c. cooked fresh or frozen)

1 c. diced celery

3 green onions, chopped

⅓ c. minced fresh parsley

DRESSING

1 c. cold water or light vegetarian broth

2 tsp. cornstarch

⅔ c. red wine vinegar

2-3 T. liquid sweetener or alternate

3 cloves garlic, crushed

2 tsp. salt

1 tsp. pepper

1 tsp. dry mustard

1 tsp. *Vegetarian Worcestershire Sauce* (p. 77)

You can make this quickly and keep it for up to a week in the refrigerator for quick lunches or a hearty addition to a green salad.

Mix the salad ingredients in a serving bowl. In a small saucepan, mix the water or broth with the cornstarch. Stir constantly over high heat until it boils, thickens, and clears. Blend with the remaining ingredients, and pour while hot over the salad ingredients. Cover and refrigerate until serving time, shaking or stirring daily if stored for a few days.

To Make Soy-Free: Use the soy-free version of *Vegetarian Wocestershire Sauce*.

Variations: If you don't have one of the beans called for, substitute another variety, such as pinto or black beans.

Pasta-Bean Salad: Omit half of the beans and substitute 3 c. cooked spiral or tube pasta. Use chopped bell pepper instead of celery, if you like.

per serving: calories: 220, protein: 10 gm., fat: 1 gm., carbohydrates: 42 gm.

oriental noodle salad

Serves 4
(can be soy-free)

THAI-STYLE NOODLE SALAD

½ lb. vermicelli pasta (whole wheat is good) or or Japanese udon noodles (buckwheat, if possible)

half a cucumber (preferably the kind with an edible peel), cut into thin strips

1 large red bell pepper, seeded and cut into strips

¼ c. chopped fresh mint, basil, or cilantro

OPTIONAL: **2 c. thinly sliced strips of seitan or grilled portobello or crimini mushrooms, *Pan-Fried "Breast of Tofu"* (p. 29), or other marinated, cooked tofu or tempeh**

¼ c. light soy sauce (or alternate, p. 13)

3 T. lime juice

2 T. sugar or alternate

1 T. chopped fresh gingerroot

1 T. pickled jalapeño pepper

1 clove garlic, peeled

2 T. toasted sesame seeds

If you add sliced seitan or an alternate, this is a full-meal salad. Lime juice and chile in the dressing makes it a Thai-style salad; rice vinegar and seaweed makes it Japanese-style.

Cook the pasta in a large pot of boiling water until tender. Meanwhile, prepare the vegetables and seitan or tofu. In a blender, mix together the soy sauce, lime juice, sugar, ginger, jalapeño, and garlic for the dressing. Drain the pasta and place in a serving bowl with the dressing and other ingredients, except the sesame seeds. Toss well. Sprinkle with the sesame seeds. Serve at room temperature. (It may be refrigerated if you aren't serving it right away.)

Japanese-Style Salad: Omit the mint, basil, or cilantro, and substitute ½ c. of shredded nori seaweed, and cut it thinly with scissors. (Get the kind you use for sushi rolls that's already toasted.) For the dressing, use rice vinegar instead of lime juice, and omit the jalapeño.

per serving: calories: 383, protein: 31 gm.,
fat: 3 gm., carbohydrates: 57 gm.

grilled vegetable salad

One of our favorite summer meals is a "grilled salad." Actually it's a green salad topped with grilled vegetables (and sometimes tofu or seitan). It's very easy to make, but comes off as "gourmet" fare!

The base of the salad is fresh, crisp greens, such as romaine lettuce. If you have any, you can add some greens with a bite, such as arugula (rocket), endive, raw kale, etc., and some shredded red cabbage, tomato wedges, and any other raw salad material you like.

Cut up anything you think would be good grilled— eggplant, summer squash, bell peppers, carrots, sweet potatoes, partially or fully-cooked potatoes, mushrooms (try the large portobellos or smaller criminis), onion, broccoli, fennel, cauliflower, tofu, tempeh, seitan, etc. (Asparagus is delicious this way!) Toss it with a bit of no-fat vinaigrette dressing—commercial or homemade. Grill these on an outdoor or indoor grill until slightly charred on all sides, or in a large, shallow pan under your stove's broiler, about 3" from the heat, stirring now and then.

Pile the grilled items on top of the bed of salad greens, and serve with more of the vinaigrette on the side. If no tofu, tempeh, or seitan was grilled, we sometimes crumble some *Marinated Tofu* (p. 30) on top too. You might also like to sprinkle the salad with a handful of chopped fresh herbs, if you have them.

Grilled Vegetable and Pasta Salad: You can also use the grilled vegetables and vinaigrette with cooked tubular or corkscrew pasta for a hearty pasta salad.

miso caesar dressing

Makes about 1¼ cups
(can be soy-free)

⅔ c. reduced-fat, medium-firm tofu, or ½ (10.5 oz.) box reduced-fat, extra-firm SILKEN tofu

¼ c. water, vegetable broth, or bean broth

¼ c. fresh lemon juice

2 T. light soy or chick-pea miso

1 T. red wine vinegar

1 tsp. Dijon mustard

2 cloves garlic, peeled

½ tsp. EACH salt and pepper

2 dashes Louisiana hot sauce

OPTIONAL: ¼ tsp. *Vegetarian Worcestershire Sauce* (p. 77)

This makes enough for two big salads. Miso takes the place of anchovies. Toss the dressing with crisp Romaine lettuce, croutons, and a little soy Parmesan.

Place all the ingredients in a blender, and process until smooth. Refrigerate.

To Make Soy-Free: Omit the tofu and water or broth, and use 1 c. soy-free *Low-Fat Mayonnaise* (p. 32). Use only ¼ tsp. salt, or to taste. Use only 3 T. lemon juice and ½ T. red wine vinegar. Omit the soy Parmesan from the salad.

per 2 tablespoons: calories: 26, protein: 2 gm., fat: 1 gm., carbohydrates: 2 gm.

thai cabbage salad

Serves 4
(can be soy-free)

SALAD
3 c. finely shredded cabbage (any type)
1 medium carrot, shredded
**1 small onion, thinly sliced (preferably a
 sweet onion)**
2 T. minced fresh cilantro or parsley
**2 T. minced fresh mint, or 2 tsp. dried
 mint**

DRESSING
2 T. light soy sauce (or alternate, p. 13)
2 T. lime or lemon juice
2 T. water or light vegetarian broth
1 T. sugar or alternate
1 T. slivered lime or lemon zest
OPTIONAL: **a pinch of kelp powder**

per serving: calories: 54, protein: 2 gm., fat: 0 gm.,
carbohydrates: 12 gm.

*This inexpensive and easy coleslaw makes a
great winter accompaniment to an Oriental
meal or spices up an otherwise mundane meal.*

Mix the salad ingredients in a serving bowl,
and add the dressing. Mix well and refrigerate
until serving time.

chapter V

pasta & pizza express

Pasta is the food of choice now for many North Americans when they want to cook up a good meal in a hurry. But, unfortunately, pasta is usually drenched in butter, olive oil, or cheese sauces, and/or topped with fatty meats and cheeses. The deliciously quick recipes in this chapter prove that you can have North America's favorite fast food without all the fat and cholesterol.

Pizza is one of our first choices for fast take-out food, but even if you choose a vegetarian pizza without cheese, the bottom crust is often drenched in oil! We offer you several very acceptable, low-fat pizza crusts (including a homemade one that you can have on the table in 25 minutes!). There are also suggestions for some delectable vegetarian toppings that are so low in fat that you won't have to make do with two little slices!

pasta

Volumes (literally!) have been written on pasta, and with good reason—pasta is delicious, nutritious, filling, satisfying, versatile, inexpensive, fat-free, and quick! Choose from a variety of dried pastas that contain no eggs (or fresh pasta made with tofu, which is available in some areas):

Italian durum semolina pasta of all shapes (including those made from whole wheat durum semolina)

Rice pastas that mimic Italian wheat pastas

Oriental rice noodles and vermicelli, cellophane, and bean thread noodles

Chinese eggless wheat noodles and Japanese udon and soba noodles (you can substitute thin Italian pastas such as spaghettini, vermicelli, or cappellini, either plain or whole wheat, for these Oriental noodles)

Broken flat Italian pasta such as linguine and fettuccine, or shapes such as small shells or bow ties, can substitute for wide egg noodles

Vermicelli or cappellini, broken, instead of fine egg noodles

Whatever pasta you choose, cook it in a large pot with LOTS of boiling, salted water (the Italian rule is 6 qts. of water per lb. of dry pasta). Cook Italian pasta until "al dente," which means "to the tooth," or tender, but still chewy. Oriental pastas should be a bit more tender, however. Oriental-style rice and starch noodles should not be boiled, but merely soaked in warm water for 15 minutes before adding to the hot dish. Drain and top or toss immediately with the sauce (but don't "drown" it!). Italians consider cold pasta "dead pasta." (Cold pasta salads are only eaten in Rome and the Italian Riviera, where there are lots of for-eigners.) Subsequently, Italians expect you to be ready and waiting when the pasta is about to be drained. It is then served from a heated, shallow pasta bowl.

Leftovers are usually used in frittatas, but they can also be added to soups. If you measure out your pasta in ounces-per-serving, you won't have a lot of leftovers. Figure 2-3 oz. for a first course and 4-6 oz. for a main course. (Italians usually eat a small portion of pasta as a separate course for the large meal of the day, but pasta as THE main course is becoming more popular.)

If you want to buck Italian convention and use up leftover pasta (I'll assume you didn't overcook it!), heat it by pouring boiling water over it in a bowl or microwaving, well-covered, for a minute or two.

To cook pasta ahead of time, use the "al segreto" method, cooking the pasta for 2 minutes less than you would to make it "al dente." Drain, but don't rinse it. When you are ready to serve, add the pasta to some of the heated sauce in a skillet, and cook it over low heat for 2 or 3 minutes; then serve in a heated bowl with more of the sauce.

Refer to Chapter IV for some speedy sauces for pasta—

Creamy Tomato Sauce (p. 71)

Golden Cheeze Sauce and variations (p. 72)

Quick Marinara Sauce (p. 76), an all-purpose tomato sauce for pasta (try adding strips of vegetarian "pepperoni," "ham," or "back bacon," vegetarian "Italian sausage" or "hamburger," or "meatballs")

Our vegan *Pesto* (p. 77)

Quick Creamy Sauce (p. 75), which can be combined with many different pastas and foods to create delicious, rich-tasting pasta dishes

pasta alla giardiniere

Serves 6
(can be soy-free)

1 lb. dry linguine, fettuccine, or
    spaghetti

1 (10.5 oz.) box firm or extra-firm lite
    SILKEN tofu

2 T. lemon juice

½ tsp. sugar or alternate

¼ tsp. salt

½ c. vegetarian broth

1 medium onion, minced

1 or 2 large cloves of garlic, minced

1 lb. thin asparagus, trimmed and cut
    diagonally into slices, or broccoli,
    cut into ¼" slices

½ lb. fresh mushrooms, sliced

1 medium zucchini or other summer
    squash, cut into ¼" rounds

1 small carrot, peeled, halved
    lengthwise, and sliced diagonally
    ⅛" thick

6 oz. cauliflower, cut into small slices

½ c. vegetarian broth

OPTIONAL: 1 T. cornstarch mixed with
    2 T. cold water

2 T. fresh basil, or 2 tsp. dried

1 c. petit pois (baby peas), or 2 c. snow
    peas, sliced 1" wide

5 green onions, chopped

salt and pepper to taste

soy Parmesan to pass at the table (omit
    for soy-free)

This is my version of pasta primavera, the famous pasta dish with spring vegetables and a creamy sauce. My version is gorgeously creamy, but almost fat-free and good enough for company!

Put the pasta on to boil in a large pot of salted water.

In a blender or food processor, blend the silken tofu, lemon juice, sugar, and salt until VERY smooth. Set aside.

In a lightly greased or nonstick skillet or wok, heat the first ½ c. of broth. When boiling, add the onions and garlic, and simmer for 2 minutes. Add the asparagus, mushrooms, cauliflower, zucchini, and carrot, and stir-fry 2-3 minutes.

Still over high heat, add the blended tofu mixture, remaining broth, and basil. Cook until the liquid thickens slightly, adding the optional dissolved cornstarch if necessary to thicken.

Add the peas and green onions to the sauce, and cook 1 minute. Taste for salt and pepper. When the pasta is al dente, drain it and add it to the sauce. Toss well and serve hot, with soy Parmesan.

Variation: Instead of steam-frying the vegetables, broil them in a large roasting pan, until they are just tender and slightly charred, using the directions for *Grilled Vegetable Salad* (p. 86). This is very quick and tastes heavenly.

To Make Soy-Free: Substitute 2 c. *Quick Creamy Sauce* (soy-free version, p. 75) for the blended tofu mixture and the broth.

per serving: calories: 190, protein: 10 gm., fat: 1 gm., carbohydrates: 34 gm.

creamy seashell casserole

Serves 4
(can be soy-free)

6 oz. medium shell pasta
1½ c. frozen peas (preferably petit pois)
2 c. sliced, fresh mushrooms (oyster
  mushrooms are good in this)
1 c. chopped onions
1 c. diced celery
1 red bell pepper, seeded and diced
½ recipe *Quick Creamy Sauce* (p. 75),
  regular or soy-free
1 T. dulse flakes
½ tsp. kelp powder
¼ c. soy Parmesan (omit for soy-free
  version)

per serving: calories: 253, protein: 16 gm.,
fat: 4 gm., carbohydrates: 37 gm.

Add the pasta to a large pot of boiling salted water. While it cooks, prepare the sauce, adding the dulse flakes and kelp powder. Steam-fry the onions, celery, mushrooms, and red pepper.

Just before the pasta is done, add the frozen peas.

Drain the pasta and peas, and mix in a shallow casserole with the vegetables and sauce. Sprinkle with the soy Parmesan, and place under the broiler just until the top is golden brown. Serve immediately.

NOTE: Pasta really soaks up this sauce as it cools, so you'll have to add a bit of water, broth, or "milk" when reheating leftovers.

pasta entrees using quick creamy sauce

You don't really need a recipe, just your imagination, to make a variety of tasty dishes with pasta of all types and *Quick Creamy Sauce* (p. 75). One recipe is enough for 2 lbs. of tossed pasta, or 1 lb., if the sauce is going to be cooked into it like a casserole.

Toss the sauce with pasta, and add:
chopped cooked (fresh or frozen) vegetables, such as frozen chopped spinach (well-squeezed), arugula, or other greens
peas
asparagus
onions and cabbage
broccoli
steam-fried mushrooms
grilled or roasted vegetables
rehydrated and sliced dried tomatoes (p. 46) and/or mushrooms
roasted peppers or rinsed marinated artichokes from a jar
strips of *Pan-Fried "Breast of Tofu"* (p. 29) or commercial marinated tofu
strips of vegetarian "deli meats" or seitan
chopped fresh parsley and other herbs
Pesto (p. 77)
vegetarian "Italian sausage," cooked and crumbled
hot tomato salsa or drained, canned diced tomatoes
strips of grilled brown mushrooms

spaghetti a la carbonnera

Toss *Quick Creamy Sauce* (p. 75) with 2 lbs. of freshly cooked spaghetti, 2 T. of soy bacon chips or ½ c. of diced vegetarian "ham" or "back bacon," and add lots of freshly ground black pepper and soy Parmesan to taste.

"straw and hay"

Use half regular and half spinach fettuccine with *Quick Creamy Sauce* (p. 75), adding a few peas, some julienned vegetarian "back bacon" or "ham," and soy Parmesan.

southwestern pasta

Mix your favorite pasta shape with *Quick Creamy Sauce* (p. 75), chopped tomatoes, canned corn, steam-fried onion, garlic, and zucchini, and some chile flakes. Another option is steam-fried or roasted bell pepper strips (any or all colors).

cabbage and noodles

Serves 4 as a main dish; 6-8 as a side dish
(can be soy-free)

2 onions, thinly sliced
½ small cabbage, shredded
1 T. chicken-style broth powder
½ tsp. salt, or to taste
freshly ground black pepper, to taste
½ lb. uncooked linguine or fettuccine
**   pasta, broken in half**
OPTIONAL: **1 tsp. caraway seeds, or 1 T.**
**   poppy seeds**
paprika to sprinkle on top

TOFU SOUR CREAM
⅓ of a (10.5 oz.) box reduced-fat, extra-
**   firm SILKEN tofu**
1 T. lemon juice
pinch EACH of salt and sugar

per serving: calories: 214, protein: 11 gm.,
fat: 3 gm., carbohydrates: 38 gm.

This Central and Eastern European dish has many versions, made with egg noodles, butter, and sour cream. This low-fat vegan version is still delicious.

Put a large pot of boiling water on for the pasta.

In a large, nonstick or lightly oiled skillet, steam-fry the onion and cabbage for about 10 minutes, or until they are tender and a bit browned. Stir in the broth powder and 2 T. water, cover, and cook over low heat. Cook the pasta in boiling water according to package directions.

To make the sour cream, blend the tofu, lemon juice, salt, and sugar in a blender or food processor until very smooth.

Over low heat, add the drained, cooked pasta and the "sour cream" to the cabbage in the skillet. Add the salt, pepper, and optional caraway or poppy seeds, and stir until well-mixed and heated through. Sprinkle with paprika and serve.

To Make Soy-Free: Use ½ c. *Soy-Free Sour Cream* (p. 33) in place of the *Tofu Sour Cream.*

pasta al pomodoro crudo
(pasta with raw tomato sauce)

Serves 3
(soy-free)

½ lb. rotelle, fusilli, rigati, rigatoni, or
    radiatore pasta
3 cloves garlic, peeled
3 T. chopped fresh basil
1 lb. (3 medium) ripe tomatoes
    (preferably plum-type), cut into
    chunks
1 tsp. salt
½ tsp. freshly ground black pepper
OPTIONAL: **6 pitted black Greek or Italian
    olives**

per serving: calories: 252, protein: 12 gm., fat: 3 gm.,
carbohydrates: 45 gm.

This is one of the fastest and most delicious recipes in the book (sort of an Italian salsa cruda), but you must have good, ripe tomatoes (preferably Italian plum tomatoes) and fresh basil. Save this for late summer meals.

Make the sauce while the pasta cooks in a large pot of boiling, salted water. Place the garlic and basil in a food processor, and pulse until finely chopped. Add the remaining ingredients and pulse quickly.

Drain the pasta and immediately toss with the uncooked sauce. Serve right away, with salad and crusty bread. (Traditionally, this is not eaten with any kind of cheese on it.)

Winter Pommodoro Crudo: This is cheating, but, if you really crave this when there aren't any good tomatoes around, use a 28-oz. can of good-quality diced tomatoes, well-drained. It still tastes pretty good with the raw garlic! If necessary, use 1 T. dry basil instead of the fresh, but you can usually find some fresh basil all year round in supermarkets.

Pasta alla Puttanesca (without the anchovies): Make the Winter version, but add ½ T. capers and ½ dried red chili pepper, crumbled. Simmer the sauce for 10 minutes.

beans and greens with pasta

Serves 4
(soy-free)

12 oz. of your favorite pasta
4 large cloves garlic, minced or crushed
2 c. arugula or other strong-flavored
greens (you can use escarole, young
kale or collards, broccoli, rabe,
mustard greens, turnip greens, etc.,
fresh or frozen), chopped or thinly
sliced
1 (14 oz.) can diced tomatoes with juice
1 (15 oz.) can drained white kidney
beans, pinto beans, or chick-peas
(1½ c. cooked)
½ c. vegetarian broth
½ c. dry white or red wine (non-
alcoholic, if preferred)
¼ c. minced fresh basil, or 1½ tsp.
dried
1 T. minced fresh sage, or 1 tsp. dried,
crumbled (not powdered)
salt and freshly ground pepper, to taste
OPTIONAL: soy Parmesan

per serving: calories: 379, protein: 18 gm.,
fat: 3 gm., carbohydrates: 69 gm.

This Tuscan-style Italian dish may become a
staple before long!

Put a large pot of salted water on to boil for
the pasta.

In a large, nonstick or lightly oiled skillet,
steam-fry the garlic for a minute. Add the
greens and steam-fry until they wilt. Add the
tomatoes, beans, broth, and wine. If using the
dried herbs, add them at this point. Simmer
while you cook the pasta to al dente (tender
but firm to the bite).

Add the fresh herbs (if using) to the sauce,
and taste for salt and pepper. Drain the pasta
and toss with the sauce. Pass the soy Parmesan,
if you wish.

szechuan noodles

Serves 5 (or 3 teenage boys!)
(can be soy-free)

1 lb. spaghettini
4 green onions, chopped
3 cloves garlic, minced
½ c. cold water
1 tsp. vegetarian broth powder (a low-salt variety)
1 tsp. cornstarch
⅓ c. soy sauce (or alternate, p. 13)
2 T. ketchup
1 T. vinegar
1 T. Szechuan hot bean paste (Chinese chile bean paste)*
1 tsp. sugar, or alternate
¼ c. chopped vegetarian "back bacon" or "ham," or 2 T. soy bacon chips or bits, soaked in 2 T. boiling water (omit for soy-free version)
¼ c. chopped, dry-roasted peanuts
⅔ c. chopped, peeled cucumber, zucchini, or celery
1 (10 oz.) pkg. frozen chopped spinach, thawed and squeezed dry**

* If you have no Chinese or Szechuan chile paste, or have a soy allergy, try Thai or Vietnamese chile paste (check for fish sauce), or even Louisiana hot sauce, but the amount may differ.

** To thaw frozen spinach quickly, cook on Hi in the microwave right in the box for 5 minutes, unwrap and or thaw under hot running water in a colander.

I've been making some version of this recipe for about 20 years. It started out with a lot of oil and a hefty portion of chopped peanuts. I substituted a slightly thickened broth for the oil, cut the amount of peanuts down by half, and added some greens. This still makes the fat count a little higher than I'd prefer, but it's such a fast and delicious meal (the number one favorite of our sons), that I know you'll forgive me this breach of the "no-peanuts" policy! (I've tried it many ways, but it just doesn't taste right without some peanuts.) It's ready in the time it takes to boil the pasta!

While the pasta cooks, heat a large, lightly greased or nonstick wok or skillet. Add and steam-fry the green onions and garlic for about 2 minutes. Mix the water, broth powder, cornstarch, soy sauce, ketchup, vinegar, chile paste, and sugar. Add this to the pan, and stir until it boils.

Add the vegetarian "ham," peanuts, cucumber, and spinach. Stir quickly over high heat until everything is hot. Drain the pasta and add to the wok or skillet. Toss quickly and serve immediately.

NOTE: To reheat leftovers, add a little water or broth, as the pasta soaks up the oil-free sauce when it cools.

per serving: calories: 238, protein: 11 gm., fat: 5 gm., carbohydrates: 38 gm.

chinese spaghetti

Serves 4
(can be soy-free)

1 lb. spaghettini
1 lb. any vegetable, cut for stir-fry (can be zucchini, broccoli, mushrooms, celery, bean sprouts, cabbage, chard, etc.)
2 green and/or red bell peppers, seeded and sliced
1 bunch green onions, or 1 large onion, diced
3 T. minced or grated fresh gingerroot
4 large cloves garlic, minced or crushed
1½ c. slivered seitan, grilled portobello or crimini mushrooms, *Pan-Fried Breast of Tofu* or *Smoky Tofu* (pps. 29-30), reconstituted textured soy protein chunks (p. 26), or commercial, cooked marinated tofu
½ c. vegetarian broth
¼ c. soy sauce
¼ c. dry sherry or non-alcoholic alternative
1 T. sugar or alternate
2 tsp. cornstarch

per serving: calories: 339, protein: 26 gm., fat: 1 gm., carbohydrates: 52 gm.

It doesn't get much easier than this! You can use any vegetable (even a package of frozen stir-fry vegetables) in this Americanized version of lo mein—and it's a "full-meal-deal."

While the pasta cooks in a large pot of boiling water, steam-fry the stir-fry vegetables, onion, ginger, and garlic in a large, very hot, lightly greased or nonstick wok or skillet. Steam-fry just until the vegetables are crisp-tender, adding the green or red pepper and the seitan or tofu towards the end.

Mix together the broth, soy sauce, sherry, sugar, and cornstarch. Pour into the pan and stir until thickened. Drain the spaghettini and add to the pan. Toss to mix well and serve.

thai-style noodle stir-fry

Serves 4
(can be soy-free)

12 oz. noodles (see comments at right)
1 c. thinly sliced broccoli florets
1 red bell pepper, seeded and sliced
1 c. trimmed snow peas, fresh or frozen
½ c. chopped cilantro, basil, or Italian parsley
¼ c. chopped green onions
⅓ c. light soy sauce (or alternate, p. 15)
OPTIONAL: ¼ tsp. kelp powder
¼ c. rice or white wine vinegar
¼ c. water
1 T. sugar or alternate
1½ tsp. minced garlic
1½ tsp. minced or grated fresh gingerroot
1 tsp. any kind of very hot Oriental chile paste (check for fish)
1 tsp. cornstarch dissolved in 1 T. water

per serving: calories: 186, protein: 8 gm.,
fat: 0 gm., carbohydrates: 37 gm.

You can be more authentic and use wide Oriental rice stick noodles, or use the equally delicious, but more accessible, linguine or fettuccine pasta in this spicy stir-fry. (Italian-style rice linguine or fettuccine pasta is also available.) If you do use the rice stick noodles, soak them in warm water for about 15 minutes, then add the soaked noodles, uncooked, to the hot stir-fry.

Add the pasta to a large pot of boiling water.

In a large, lightly oiled or nonstick wok or skillet, cover and steam the broccoli in 2 T. water for 3 minutes. Add the red pepper, snow peas, and cilantro, and steam for 1-2 minutes. Add the remaining ingredients (except the cornstarch), and bring to a boil. Add the dissolved cornstarch and stir until thickened. Drain the pasta and add it to the hot mixture; toss well and serve immediately.

Variations: You can substitute other vegetables, if you like. You can also add slivers of leftover tofu, seitan, textured vegetable protein, etc.

pizza crusts

The best pizza starts with a good crust. Some good choices are:

1. A commercial, prebaked pizza crust (also called an Italian flat bread or focaccia), white or whole wheat. Some have cheese melted on them, but they are available plain or with herbs. Add your toppings and bake at 450°F for 10 minutes.

2. Unsplit pita bread (as thick or as thin as you like it, depending on the brand), white or whole wheat. Add toppings and bake as above.

3. French or Italian crusty bread, sourdough or plain, whole wheat or white. Cut long loaves in half lengthwise, add the toppings, and bake as above.

4. Frozen BREAD dough (not frozen pizza crust). Take out of the freezer in the morning to thaw, or thaw in a plastic bag in the microwave on LOW for 6 minutes for a loaf or 3 minutes for rolls. Bake as instructed for *Quick Pizza Dough* (p. 99).

5. *Quick Pizza Dough*, (p. 99). You can also make a very good homemade crust in your food processor, using quick-rise baking yeast. (This is the cheapest by far.)

quick pizza dough

Makes one 14" pizza or 2 (8") "pizzettes"
(can be soy-free)

1⅓ c. unbleached white flour
⅔ c. whole wheat flour (or unbleached white)
2 T. soymilk or other nondairy "milk" powder
1 T. quick-rising baking yeast
1 tsp. salt
½ tsp. sugar or Sucanat, or 1 tsp. granulated alternate
¾-1 c. hot water

per serving: calories: 111, protein: 5 gm., fat: 0 gm., carbohydrates: 22 gm.

You can have homemade pizza on the table in 25 minutes if you have a food processor.

Preheat the oven to 500°F.

Combine the flours, "milk" powder, yeast, salt, and sugar in a food processor. With the motor running, add ¾ c. hot water. The dough should form a ball on the top of the blade. If it doesn't, add the remaining water, 1 T. at a time, until it does. Process for 1 minute. Remove the dough to a floured surface, knead briefly, cover, and let rest 10 minutes.

While the dough rests, prepare your toppings (facing page).

Roll out the dough to fit a lightly oiled or nonstick 14" pizza pan, leaving a "rim." Add your toppings and bake 10-12 minutes (6-8 minutes for pizzettes).

Focaccia: To make this bread treat, make indentations all over the rolled-out dough with your finger tips, then spread thinly with tomato sauce, crushed tomatoes, non-fat vinaigrette, or *Pesto* (p. 77). Top with herbs, chopped garlic or garlic granules, onions, soy Parmesan, etc., and bake as above.

pizza toppings

The Sauce: For fast pizza, your best bet is a good-quality, commercial pizza or marinara (tomato) sauce. You can even buy excellent organic brands in natural foods stores. I like a chunky sauce, but, if you prefer a smooth one, a can of Italian-style tomato sauce will do the trick. Experiment with mushroom or vegetable and tomato sauces too.

Instead of a sauce, you can use canned, crushed or pureed tomatoes, drained, canned diced tomatoes, or sliced, fresh plum tomatoes. Just sprinkle them with salt and pepper, fresh or dried herbs, and crushed or minced garlic.

Whatever you use for a sauce, don't spread it too thickly.

---

cheese or not?

You don't HAVE to put cheese (or cheeze) on a pizza—in Italy, a pizza is not always made with cheese, and even when it is, Italians use less than North Americans do.

I prefer not to use cheese substitutes on pizza, except perhaps for a sprinkle of soy Parmesan, but you can use a low-fat vegan cheese substitute if you like. Crumbled *Marinated Tofu* (p. 30) adds a Greek touch. A thin drizzling of *Melty Pizza Cheeze* (p. 42) does the trick for many former cheese fans.

The Toppings
Your choice of:
raw, sliced, or steam-fried onions
raw or roasted, sliced bell peppers (any color
soaked, sliced dried tomatoes (p. 15)
grilled or roasted eggplant, zucchini, or portobello or crimini mushrooms
artichoke hearts
raw or steam-fried mushrooms
soaked, dried sliced mushrooms
chopped raw or roasted garlic
Pesto (p. 77)
chile flakes
chopped, raw arugula
chopped, raw or squeezed, frozen or cooked spinach or other greens
fresh herbs
vegetarian "pepperoni," "Italian sausage," "sausage," or "burger" (p. 28,) "back bacon," or "ham"
steamed or roasted asparagus
strips of *Pan-Fried Breast of Tofu* or *Smoky Pan-Fried Tofu* (pps. 29-30), or commercial marinated tofu or tempeh
strips of seitan or reconstituted textured vegetable protein chunks (p. 26)
smoked tofu
anything else that sounds good

You can also experiment with "fusion" pizza—for example:

Mexican: Tomato salsa or taco sauce, black beans or *Spicy Bean Dip* (p. 50), crumbled vegetarian "burger," corn, green chiles, cilantro, etc.

Middle Eastern: Sliced or diced tomatoes with garlic and oregano, bits of *Marinated Tofu* (p. 30), artichokes, etc.

Chinese: Tomato sauce flavored with hoisin sauce and Szechuan hot bean paste, shiitake mushrooms, peppers, green onions, and shredded marinated tofu or mun chai'ya, the canned Chinese vegetarian "roast duck"

Indian: Spread with leftover tomato-based curry, such as *Mattar Tofu* (p. 130).

"Galette" (a French savory pie): Top small rounds of dough, small prebaked pizza shells, or pita breads with one of these:
  quick-roasted onions and/or garlic (p. 44)
  bottled vegetarian antipasto
  Pesto (p. 77)
Top with one or all of these:
  steamed, roasted, grilled, or broiled
    vegetables
  bits of veggie "back bacon," "ham," or
    "pepperoni"
  crumbled *Marinated Tofu* (p. 30)
  soy Parmesan;
  cherry tomato halves
  Tofu Ricotta (p. 34)
  perhaps a couple of chopped olives

NOTE: If you have a tomato allergy, make a "White Pizza," and just leave out the tomato!

5-minute tortilla "pizza"

If you're REALLY in a hurry, try making quick "pizza" in your microwave using flour tortillas for a thin crust. For each "pizza," pierce an 8" low-fat flour tortilla in several places with a fork (so that it won't puff up). Brush with water on both sides. Put the tortilla between two sheets of paper towelling on a microwaveable plate. Cook at full power for 45 seconds. If it is not dry to the touch and almost crisp (it firms more as it cools), cook longer, in 10 second increments, until it is—but don't overcook or it will become hard. Place the tortilla on a plate, and add toppings (see previous page). Microwave at full power about 1 minute, and serve.

To cook in a regular oven, crisp on a cookie sheet at 500°F for 4 minutes, add toppings, then bake 2 minutes longer.

"salad pizza"

Bake the pizza dough plain (puncture dough all over with a fork before baking), then top artistically with tomato slices, artichoke hearts, lettuce, and other salad vegetables, perhaps *Marinated Tofu* (p. 30), and vegetarian deli slices. Drizzle with vinaigrette.

greek-style spinach "pizza"

Serves 6

1 (12") prebaked pizza or Italian flat bread crust (If you prefer, you can prepare a *Quick Pizza Dough* crust, p. 100)Spinach;Pizza, Greek Style

FILLING
¾ lb. (12 oz. or 1½ c.) reduced-fat, medium-firm tofu, or 1½ (10.5 oz.) boxes reduced-fat, extra-firm SILKEN tofu
2 T. light miso
1 T. nutritional yeast flakes
1 (10 oz.) pkg. frozen chopped spinach, thawed and squeezed dry
⅔ c. finely chopped green onion stems (green part only)
1 T. dry dillweed, or ¼ c. chopped fresh
½ tsp. salt
OPTIONAL: slices of red bell pepper to decorate the top

per serving: calories: 235, protein: 14 gm., fat: 3 gm., carbohydrates: 37 gm.

This rather original "pizza" is a deliciously quick way to get the taste of spanikopita without all the messing around with phyllo pastry. Miso, tofu, and nutritional yeast give this filling an authentic feta-like flavor. You can use this filling to make actual vegan spanikopitas when you have time.*

Preheat the oven to 450°F. Mix the tofu, miso, and nutritional yeast together in a bowl with a potato masher. (DO NOT blend or process.) Add the remaining ingredients and mix together well. Spread the filling evenly over the crust. Decorate with red pepper slices, if you like. Bake on a nonstick or lightly oiled cookie sheet for 15 minutes.

* This amount of filling will fill 10 small triangles, 7 rolls, an 8" square spanikopita, or a 9"-10" filled pie or open-faced quiche. Double the recipe for a 9" x 13" pan of spanikopita, 2 pies or quiches, 20 triangles, or 14 rolls. You can add a third package of spinach to the double recipe of filling, if you like it more "green."

quick tip
Quick-thaw frozen spinach by microwaving on HI right in the box for 5 minutes, or unwrap and run under hot tap water in a colander until thoroughly thawed.

quiche pizza

Serves 6

1 (12") prebaked pizza or Italian flat bread crust (or you can prepare a *Quick Pizza Dough* crust, p. 100)

FILLING
1 lb. reduced-fat, medium-firm tofu, or 2 (10.5 oz.) boxes reduced-fat, extra-firm SILKEN tofu
3 T. nutritional yeast flakes
1 T. light miso
½ T. lemon juice
¾ tsp. salt
¼ tsp. EACH garlic granules, turmeric, and white pepper
pinch EACH of nutmeg, cayenne, and ground mustard powder
2 T. soy bacon chips, or ¼-½ c. chopped vegetarian "back bacon" or "ham," smoked tofu or *Smoky Tofu*, (p. 30), or vegetarian "pepperoni"
2 T. dried onion flakes, or 1 large onion or leek, chopped and steam-fried
2 T. soy Parmesan

This is made the same way as Greek-Style Spinach Pizza (p. 103) but with a vegan quiche filling. You can use this filling to make a regular 10" quiche when you have the time—bake at 350°F for 55 minutes.

Preheat the oven to 450°F. To make the filling, mash the tofu, soymilk, nutritional yeast, miso, lemon juice, salt, and spices in a bowl with a potato masher. (DO NOT blend or process.) Add the soy bacon chips or alternate and onion flakes.

Spread filling evenly over the crust. Sprinkle with soy Parmesan and bake for 15 minutes.

per serving: calories: 268, protein: 19 gm., fat: 5 gm., carbohydrates: 38 gm.

Variations:

You can top the filling (before adding the soy Parmesan) with:

½ c. of cooked or leftover vegetables

herbs (up to 1 T.)

To the filling, you can use combinations such as:

dill and basil with mushrooms and red peppers

corn, green peppers or zucchini,

green   chiles or jalapeños, and oregano

corn and green onions

mushrooms

mushrooms and broccoli

artichoke hearts and dried tomatoes

leafy greens with dill, chives, and basil

all colors of bell peppers

zucchini, marjoram or *Pesto* (p. 77), and roma tomatoes or red pepper

parsley and lemon zest

Grilled Eggplant (p. 107) or other grilled vegetables (p. 86)

For a more "feta-like" taste, use 2 T. miso and ½ tsp. salt.

chapter VI
fast food tonight!
burgers, patties, grills & rapid wraps

Grilling is trendy, but it also makes sense for vegetarian cooks with an eye on the clock. Almost any food can be grilled using a commercial or homemade marinade, barbecue sauce, glaze, or fat-free vinaigrette. Lemon juice and balsamic vinegar vinaigrettes are particularly good, but vinaigrettes made from flavored gourmet vinegars, such as herb, fruit, sherry, etc., also make good bastes. Grilled foods have extra flavor—that smoky taste that we just can't seem to get enough of. And it's fast! Most vegetarian grillables don't need a lot of cooking, so what you're actually doing is searing the outside of the food to keep the yummy juices in and just heating the insides.

By "grilling," I don't necessarily mean cooking over an outdoor, or even an indoor, grill or barbecue. I most often "grill" in the broiler of my stove. Or you can use a specially grooved grill skillet that you can use on top of the stove. You can add a few drops of liquid smoke to your marinade or glaze, if you like.

Slight charring is expected with this type of cooking, but don't overdo it. Charred meat and animal fat contain copious carcinogens; charred vegetable products contain a few as well.

Some of the following recipes are simply cooked in a skillet on your stovetop, but many can be reheated over a grill or under a broiler for extra flavor and verve. If the item falls apart easily, use a special rack with small holes, sometimes called a "Griffo Grill."

And, by the way, even though marinating usually involves planning ahead, these recipes offer a method of "quick-marinating" by simmering the food in the marinade for 5 minutes before grilling to allow the food to absorb the marinade without waiting.

The preferred method is to allow the food to soak in the marinade for several hours or days. This is actually a convenience. If you have tofu, textured vegetable protein chunks, seitan, or other foods soaking in several marinades in your refrigerator all the time, you have the makings for some very tasty fast-food meals!

simply delicious grilled eggplant

Slice a firm eggplant into ½"-thick slices. Dip each slice into a mixture of 1 part soy sauce (or alternate, p. 13) and 1 part balsamic vinegar, with a few shakes of liquid smoke.

Broil or grill until browned on both sides, or bake on lightly greased or nonstick dark cookie sheets at 400°F until browned on both sides.

Variation: Instead of the soy sauce-vinegar mixture, use any tasty, no-fat vinaigrette dressing or marinade, such as *Balsamic Vinaigrette* (p. 81) or *Teriyaki Marinade* (p. 108).

The eggplant is good hot or cold, in sandwiches, salads, or as a side dish.

See also *Grilled Vegetable Salad* (p. 86) for directions on grilling or broiling vegetables.

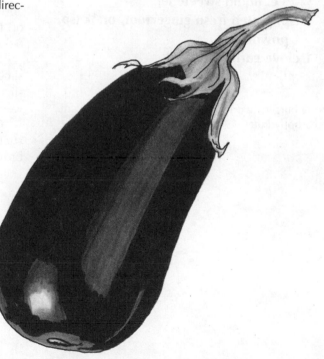

teriyaki tofu burgers

makes about 8 burgers
(can be soy-free)

1½ lbs. reduced-fat, firm tofu, sliced
  ¼" thick

TERIYAKI MARINADE
½ c. EACH water and soy sauce (or
  alternate, p. 13)
¼ c. dry sherry or white wine (or apple,
  pineapple, or white grape juice)
¼-⅓ c. liquid sweetener
1 tsp. grated fresh gingerroot, or ¼ tsp.
  powdered
1 clove garlic, crushed

per burger: calories: 138, protein: 11 gm., fat: 4 gm., carbohydrates: 13 gm.

Serve these like "cutlets" or burgers on sesame buns, slice them up and eat in a wheat tortilla, or add to a stir-fry. This marinade can also be used with reconstituted textured vegetable protein chunks and commercial, "chickeny" burgers and cutlets (including soy-free varieties).

Mix together the marinade ingredients in a small pot, and simmer for a few minutes over high heat.

To use right away, cover the tofu slices with the marinade in a nonstick or lightly oiled skillet. Simmer at medium-high heat for about 5 minutes so that the tofu absorbs some of the marinade. Then cook as instructed below.

To use later, pour the sauce over the tofu slices in a covered container, covering the slices with the sauce. Refrigerate for up to a week.

Grill or broil the slices, or pan-fry in a nonstick skillet over medium-high heat until browned on both sides.

catalán-style grill in garlic-cumin sauce

Serves 4-6
(can be soy-free)

MARINADE

⅓ c. vinaigrette made with red wine vinegar or sherry vinegar (You can use the Balsamic Vinaigrette recipe (p. 81), but replace the balsamic vinaigrette with sherry vinegar or red wine vinegar.)
2-3 T. liquid sweetener*
2 tsp. ground cumin
2 cloves garlic, crushed
½ tsp. salt

¾-1 lb. reduced-fat, extra-firm tofu, cut into 48 cubes (or see suggested substitutes in comments at right)
6 bamboo skewers, soaked in water for 15 minutes

*Do not use molasses or barley malt syrup.

per serving: calories: 130, protein: 10 gm., fat: 4 gm., carbohydrates: 12 gm.

Skewers of extra-firm tofu replace chicken in this luscious marinade inspired by a recipe from Catalonia, Spain. The tofu can also be replaced by tempeh, a light seitan, reconstituted textured vegetable protein chunks (p. 26), or canned Chinese gluten "roast duck" (mun chai' ya).

Mix together the marinade ingredients.

If you want to cook the tofu cubes right away, simmer them in the marinade in a non-stick or lightly oiled skillet over medium-high heat for 5 minutes to absorb some of the marinade.

If using later, mix the tofu cubes with the marinade to cover, and refrigerate several hours or days until ready to grill.

Thread the marinated tofu onto the skewers (8 cubes per skewer), and grill, broil, or barbecue about 3"-4" from the heat source until slightly charred on all sides. Serve on a bed of steamed, long grain rice with romaine lettuce and orange salad.

NOTE: If you have cubes of extra-firm tofu marinating in *Breast of Tofu Marinade* (p. 29), you can use them instead of plain tofu.

grilled yakitori skewers

Serves 8
(can be soy-free)

YAKITORI GLAZE
¾ c. soy sauce (or alternate, p. 13)
¾ c. dry sherry or mirin (Japanese rice wine) or non-alcoholic alternate
4½ T. sugar or alternate
3 T. cornstarch mixed with ⅓ c. cold water

16 bamboo skewers (soaked in water for 15 minutes)
1½ lbs. reduced-fat, extra-firm tofu (see suggested substitutes in comments above right)
32 small, fresh button mushrooms (preferably brown ones)
16 green onions, trimmed to include only 3" of the green stems and cut into 1½" lengths

per serving: calories: 168, protein: 13 gm., fat: 4 gm., carbohydrates: 19 gm.

Traditional yakitori are little skewers of chicken and chicken liver with a sticky, Japanese soy glaze. Here we do the same with chunks of extra-firm tofu and mushrooms. You could substitute tempeh, reconstituted textured vegetable protein chunks, lightly-flavored seitan, or mun chai'ya, the canned Chinese vegetarian "roast duck" made from wheat gluten, for the tofu, if you like. This makes great fare for a barbecue or picnic.

You can purchase bamboo skewers in most large supermarkets or hardware stores, Oriental grocery stores, or cookware shops.

Cut each ½ lb. of tofu into 24 cubes. Mix the soy sauce, sugar, and wine. If you want to grill them right away, simmer the tofu cubes with the marinade in a nonstick or lightly oiled skillet on medium-high heat for about 5 minutes, to absorb some of the marinade.

If using later, refrigerate the tofu cubes in the marinade for several hours or days, stirring or shaking once in a while.

When ready to cook, thread the marinated tofu cubes on the soaked skewers alternately with the mushrooms and green onion pieces. Each skewer should hold 5 tofu cubes, 3 mushrooms, and 3 green onion pieces. Two skewers will have 6 tofu cubes each.

Pour the remaining marinade into a small pot, and add the dissolved cornstarch and water. Stir over high heat until the sauce thickens and boils.

Brush the skewers with the sauce, and grill or broil about 3"-4" from the heat source until glazed and slightly charred on all sides, basting with the glaze when you turn the skewers. They will take only about 7 minutes to cook.

Serve the skewers immediately, 2 per person. Steamed rice and vegetables (fresh or frozen) complete the meal.

spur of the moment kebabs

Follow the recipe for Yakitori, but use any barbecue sauce or glaze that you like instead of the Yakitori Glaze. You can use the *Balsamic Vinaigrette* (p. 81), the *Red Chile and Orange Barbecue Sauce* (p. 71), or your favorite homemade or commercial sauce—even a flavorful, fat-free vinaigrette works.

Instead of, or in addition to, the mushrooms and green onions, you can use small, partly-cooked red potatoes, bell pepper squares, small quartered onions, eggplant or zucchini chunks, pineapple chunks, etc.

You can use chunks of tempeh, light seitan, reconstituted textured vegetable protein chunks (p. 26), and/or mun chai' ya (Chinese canned gluten "roast duck") in addition to, or instead of, the tofu cubes.

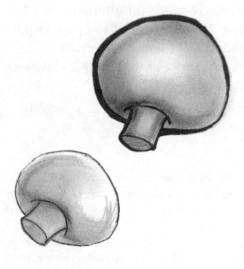

four-way glazed seitan or textured vegetable protein chunks

Serves 4
(can be soy-free)

3 c. (¾" x 1" x ¼") light seitan chunks, or 2 c. dry textured vegetable protein chunks (p. 26), reconstituted

KOREAN BARBECUE SAUCE
½ c. soy sauce (or alternate, p. 13)
¼ c. water
2 green onions, chopped
3 T. sugar or alternate
2 T. hulled sesame seeds
2 T. cornstarch
2 large cloves garlic, peeled
¼ tsp. black pepper

per serving: calories: 262, protein: 38 gm., fat: 3 gm., carbohydrates: 21 gm.

BLACK BEAN SAUCE
⅓ c. water
⅓ c. Chinese black bean sauce (or soy-free alternate, p. 13)
3 T. dry sherry or white wine
3 T. vinegar
3-4 T. liquid sweetener
6-10 cloves garlic, peeled
2 tsp. cornstarch

per serving: calories: 386, protein: 38 gm., fat: 1 gm., carbohydrates: 46 gm.

SHERRY GLAZE
1 small onion, chopped
6 T. water
6 T. soy sauce (or alternate, p. 13)
⅓ c. dry sherry
¼ c. Sucanat or brown sugar
1 T. cornstarch
4 cloves garlic, peeled

per serving: calories: 254, protein: 36 gm., fat: 1 gm., carbohydrates: 20 gm.

JALAPEÑO OR HOT RED PEPPER JELLY GLAZE
⅓ c. wine (dry white, dry sherry, or dry vermouth) or juice
⅓ c. soy sauce (or alternate, p. 13)
⅓ c. jalapeño or hot red pepper jelly
¼-⅓c. light liquid sweetener
½ tsp. garlic granules, or 2 cloves garlic, crushed

per serving: calories: 337, protein: 36 gm., fat: 1 gm., carbohydrates: 42 gm.

These delicious glazes turn humble seitan or textured vegetable protein chunks into company fare. (Extra-firm tofu, tempeh, or mun chai'ya, the canned Chinese vegetarian "roast duck" made from wheat gluten, can also be treated this way.) They are reminiscent of Oriental-style barbecued "ribs." Serve them with steamed rice, or in hot pita pockets, low-fat wheat tortillas, or Mandarin pancakes.

To make any of the sauces, combine the ingredients in a blender for a few minutes.

You can "quick-marinate" by cooking the chunks in the sauce for 5 minutes at a simmer.

If using later, marinate the vegetable protein chunks or seitan in the sauce or glaze of your choice for several hours or days.

Otherwise, just mix the sauce with the textured vegetable protein or seitan, and spread the mixture on 1 large or 2 smaller, nonstick or lightly greased cookie sheets. Place under the broiler, about 4" from the heat, and broil on one side for 5 minutes, or until slightly charred. Turn everything over with a spatula, and broil the other side for another 5 minutes, or until slightly charred.

If you prefer kebabs, thread the marinated chunks on bamboo skewers that have been soaked in cold water for 15 minutes, and grill, barbecue, or broil them until slightly charred on all sides. Use the remaining sauce to baste the kebabs. You can alternate the chunks with pieces of onion, green pepper, mushroom, pineapple, eggplant, etc.

---

glazed tofu chunks or strips

This makes either a great, quick appetizer (with a toothpick in each cube, or threaded on bamboo skewers with pineapple and green pepper chunks), or a main dish served over rice, or in pita pockets or tortillas.

Simply cut a block of reduced-fat, extra-firm tofu into small chunks or strips. Brown them on all sides in a nonstick skillet. (It's okay if they get slightly charred in places.) Then almost cover with some sort of sticky glaze or barbecue sauce (any of the ones in this chapter, *Red Chile and Orange Barbecue Sauce* (p. 71), or your favorite. Use ¾ to 1½ c. of sauce for 12-14 oz. of tofu. Cook over high heat, stirring, until the chunks get saturated

and a bit sticky with the glaze.

You can also use *Mole Sauce* (p. 134) in this way.

grilled "steak-style" mushrooms

There are a number of mushroom varieties that are excellent when grilled. Portobello mushrooms are actually a very large version of the domestic, cultivated brown mushroom (which is sometimes called a "crimini"), but they have a meaty texture and a rich flavor reminiscent of European mushrooms. Portobellos are often as big as a small steak—and can be served instead of one! You can use either crimini, portobello, oyster, or fresh shiitake instead of the hard-to-find and very expensive fresh porcini or cèpes.

To grill, barbecue, or broil them, wash them JUST before cooking pat them dry with paper towels, and remove the stems (Chop the stems for use in other dishes.) Brush them with a very garlicky, no-fat vinaigrette dressing or light marinade, such as *Balsamic Vinaigrette* (p. 81). Lemon mixtures are also delicious. Grill or broil on a rack about 4" from the heat source for about 6 minutes per side, or until very tender and juicy when pierced and very well browned on the outside.

Grilled portobellos can be sliced and used instead of meat, textured vegetable protein chunks, or seitan in many recipes. When I call for "brown mushrooms," you can use crimini, portobello, or fresh shiitake.

soy *"fish cakes"*

Makes 20

1 lb. frozen, reduced-fat, medium-firm tofu, thawed, well squeezed, and finely crumbled
2 c. cooked short grain brown rice
1 small onion, minced
6 T. nutritional yeast flakes
2 T. minced celery

BLENDED MIXTURE
¼ lb. reduced-fat, medium-firm tofu
2½ T. soy sauce
2 T. water
1 T. lemon juice
1 T. herbal salt, or 2 T. light miso
1 tsp. kelp powder
½ tsp. EACH dry mustard and dillweed
¼ tsp. white pepper
pinch celery seed

¼ c. unbleached flour or vital wheat gluten powder

each: calories: 63, protein: 6 gm., fat: 1 gm., carbohydrates: 8 gm.

These "cakes" are very tasty, with a mild seafood flavor, and they are a good way to use up that last 2 c. of leftover cooked rice. The plain ones make great "fish burgers," served on buns. I've also included some exotic flavor options. Freeze any leftovers (the uncooked mixture or the cooked patties) for future meals.

Mix the frozen tofu, rice, onion, yeast, and celery in a large bowl. Combine the Blended Mixture ingredients in a blender or food processor until smooth. Add this to the bowl, along with the flour. Mix well with your hands. (You can make this ahead of time, and refrigerate it until you are ready to cook the patties.)

Form 20 thin patties and cook in a nonstick skillet over medium-low heat about 6 minutes per side, covering the skillet while cooking the first side.

Or place the patties on lightly greased or nonstick cookie sheets, and bake at 400°F for 7 minutes per side.

To make a crunchy outside coating on the patties, coat them with *Seasoned Coating Mix* (p. 45), and bake using the oven method described above. Serve "fish cakes" alone, or on buns or toast, with *Tartar Sauce* (p. 33), ketchup, or chile sauce.

The mixture can also be shaped like "fish sticks," if you like, instead of patties.

Thai "Fish Cakes": Add 1 T. Thai red chile paste, 4 cloves crushed garlic, and ½ c. chopped green beans or peas to the tofu-rice mixture. Top with a vinegar sauce made by mixing ½ c. vinegar, ⅓ c. minced onion, 2 T. sugar, 2 T. minced fresh basil or cilantro, 2 T. grated carrot, and 1 small dried red chile, crushed.

Indian-Style "Fish Cakes": Add 2 T. grated fresh gingerroot, 2 T. minced cilantro, 1 T. minced fresh mint, 2 cloves crushed garlic, and a pinch EACH of curry powder, cayenne, turmeric, coriander, and red chile pepper flakes to the tofu-rice mixture.

Jamaican-Style "Fish Cakes": Add 2 T. chopped jalapeño and 2 tsp. paprika to the tofu-rice mixture.

Cajun-Style "Fish Cakes": Add ½ c. minced green onion, 2 tsp. Cajun seasoning, and 2 crushed cloves of garlic.

rapid wraps

the bread or wrapper

breads and buns

Any of our traditional North American breads make good sandwiches, but look beyond good old white, whole wheat, or rye slices. Try English muffins, bagels, crusty French or Italian bread or rolls, sourdough, rye crisp, or kaiser buns. If you live in a big city, check out ethnic bakeries for different kinds of breads and buns. Even if you use the same old fillings, they'll seem like a new food when served in a variety of breads.

You can wrap flatbreads from the four corners of the world around your favorite, everyday or exotic fillings. Tortillas, pitas, naan, chapatis, Beijing pancakes, Lebanese wrapper bread or lavash—the staple breads of many countries can add flair and flavor to the North American fast-food diet!

---

vegetarian heros, subs, gyros, hoagies, po' boys, and tortas

Use the best crusty rolls you can find or an oblong loaf of good, crusty French, Italian, or sourdough bread, cut in half lengthwise. If you're really planning to stuff them, pull out some of the soft inside dough and save for bread crumbs.

Moisten the inside of the bun or bread with no-fat vinaigrette dressing, *Russian Dressing* (p. 33), mayonnaise (see flavored versions on p. 33), or even barbecue sauce.

Fill with sliced roma tomatoes, red onion, romaine lettuce or other greens, such as arugula or radicchio), grilled eggplant (p. 107), and peppers (p. 44).

If you like, add:
  parsley or other fresh herbs
  mashed roasted garlic (p. 44)
  soaked dried tomatoes (p. 46)
  gourmet mustard
  Pesto (p. 77)
  coleslaw or sauerkraut
  pepperoncini (Italian pickled peppers)
  prepared horseradish
  steam-fried or grilled portobellos or any brown
      mushrooms (p. 113)
  thinly sliced seitan
  smoked tofu or *Smoky Tofu* (p. 30)
  commercial "deli slices"

Mexican "Tortas": Spread crusty rolls with cold *Spicy Bean Dip* (p. 50) or mashed beans, and add salsa, shredded lettuce, and *Tofu Sour Cream* (p. 35), *Tofu-Cashew Sour Cream* (p. 36), or *Soy-Free Sour Cream* (p. 33). Vegetarian "deli slices" and/or *Marinated Tofu Cubes* (p. 30) or smoked tofu are optional. You could also add some canned chiles, if you like them, or mix some smoky, canned chipotle chiles into the "sour cream," beans, or salsa.

New Orleans-Style Peacemaker or "Oyster" Po' Boy: Fill a crusty, hollowed-out loaf with steam-fried or grilled oyster mushrooms (p. 113), seasoned with cayenne pepper, and garnish with *Tartar Sauce* (p. 33), sliced tomatoes, and lettuce.

"French-Dip" Sandwich: Fill a crusty roll with thinly sliced seitan or grilled portobello or crimini mushrooms (p. 113), and serve with the seitan cooking juice, mushroom broth (made with a commercial mushroom broth cube), or a "beefy" broth made from hot water, soy sauce, and yeast extract to taste. Serve hot mustard or prepared horseradish on the side.

"Meatball Sub": Fill a loaf or roll with commercial or homemade vegetarian "meatballs" or *"Italian Sausage"* (p. 28), and hot, spicy tomato sauce, with or without roasted peppers (p. 44) and onions.

Chicago-Style Italian "Beef" or "Sausage" Sandwich: Fill a crusty roll (moistened with tofu or low-fat mayonnaise) with thinly sliced, juicy seitan or grilled portobello or crimini mushrooms, seasoned with oregano, black pepper, and red chile pepper flakes. You can also add thin slices of vegetarian *"Italian Sausage"* (p. 28). Top with roasted peppers (p. 44) or giardiniera, an Italian pepper relish that you can buy in a jar.

New Orleans-Style Muffuletta: Use a whole loaf of crusty French or Italian bread (round loaf preferred), cut it horizontally, and pull out the soft bread inside. Moisten with a no-fat vinaigrette full of garlic, parsley, and black pepper. Fill the hollowed-out loaf with vegetarian "back bacon" or "ham," thinly sliced seitan or grilled portobello or crimini mushrooms, sliced roma tomatoes and red onions, and shredded lettuce. Top with the other half of the loaf, and cut into quarters.

flatbreads

We're all familiar with tortillas (both flour and corn) and pita bread, but there are many more flatbreads that make delicious wraps. Many of the more exotic ones (to us, anyway) would have to be homemade, but we can use more easily available substitutes. Here's a sampling of some of these flatbreads, with suggestions for substitutes.

Beijing pancakes, Mandarin pancakes, la ta, or Chinese tortillas: very thin, tortilla-like flatbreads, cooked in a double layer, and separated before using as a wrapper for grills and stir-fries. Substitute very thin, small white flour tortillas.

Chapati: unleavened, whole wheat flat breads from India, Pakistan, and the Caribbean, eaten with spicy grills and curries. Substitute whole wheat tortillas.

Focaccia: leavened Italian flat bread, a little thicker than pizza dough, usually seasoned with herbs. Use for open-faced vegetable sandwiches; substitute naan.

Lavash or lavosh: Lebanese or Armenian leavened flat bread for wrapping around felafel, vegetables, etc.; fresh is preferable. You can substitute large, thin flour tortillas.

Nan or naan: leavened flat bread from Central Asia, baked on the walls of a tandoor oven, used for wrapping grilled foods; substitute plain focaccia.

Pita: round, leavened white or whole wheat bread from the Middle East, cooked at high heat so that a pocket forms inside to fill with grilled foods, salads, vegetables, felafel, etc. You can substitute wheat tortillas or lavash, though they don't have pockets. Pita can also be used as a low-fat substitute for Southwestern or Navajo "fry bread," or fried Nepalese breads used for stuffing. It can be stuffed with fillings that you would use in filled bread doughs or pastries.

Norwegian potato lefse: unleavened potato and wheat flat bread, for making rolled sandwiches; substitute wheat tortillas.

Tortillas: round, unleavened wheat or corn flatbreads from Mexico, Central America, and the American Southwest, topped, rolled, and filled in many different ways. Substitute lavash, chapati, Norwegian potato lefse, pita, or Beijing pancakes.

rolled and wrapped sandwiches

Almost any sandwich filling can be rolled up in a flat bread instead of served between two slices of bread. Your best bets for rolled and spiral sandwiches are flour tortillas and fresh Lebanese wrapping bread or lavash.

Spread each round bread with either a *Tofu Cream "Cheese"* (p. 36) or a commercial brand, or tofu mayonnaise or low-fat mayonnaise (pps. 31-32). Try the flavored mayos on p. 33. You can add gourmet mustard too, if you like. Next, arrange your filling (something flat, thin, and flexible) to within ½" of the edges. Roll up like a jelly roll, and cut in half or into thick slices for spirals. You can make the sandwich rolls several hours ahead if the filling isn't too moist and the rolls are well wrapped in plastic.

Possible fillings for rolled sandwiches:
alfalfa sprouts or other soft, fresh sprouts, or watercress (these roll better than lettuce)
a leaf of crisp romaine (place along the side you start to roll with)
fresh herbs (basil, cilantro, parsley, etc.)
vegetarian deli "meats"
very thinly sliced cooked *Pan-Fried Breast of Tofu* or *Smoky Tofu* (pps. 29-30)
very thinly sliced seitan or grilled portobello or crimini mushrooms
thin slices of grilled eggplant (p. 107) or peppers (p. 44)
Hummus (p. 51) or other thick bean spread
thinly sliced sweet onion
grated carrots and/or radishes

If you are going to eat the sandwich in 2 hours or less, you can use thinly sliced cucumbers, roma tomatoes, and moist fillings such as *Mock Tuna* (p. 127), *Eggless Egg Salad* (p. 126), minced vegetarian "ham," or *Pan Fried "Breast of Tofu"* (p. 29) mixed with low-fat mayonnaise. You could add some green onion, green pepper, and curry powder.

For wrapped sandwiches, use flour tortillas which can be served cold or warm, or corn tortillas, served warm. Just spread filling down the middle, fold up the bottom to catch drips, and wrap the sides over. You can use any sandwich filling or hearty salad, hot or cold. You can also try something as simple as steamed, grilled, or steam-fried vegetables (with or without a sauce), or use a grill, stir-fry, a curry, stew, chile, etc. (see Chapters VII and VIII). If you like, serve some accompaniments with the filling, such as shredded lettuce or cabbage, sliced cucumbers, peppers, tomatoes, grated carrot, sprouts, etc.

mexican-style tortilla wraps

Mexican wraps get their own section because there are so many variations, and they are so universally loved! Tostadas (single and stacked), enchiladas, soft tacos, burritos, chimichangas, quesadillas, fajitas— they're all delicious!

If you don't have homemade beans or sauces handy, use canned beans or instant dried bean flakes (p. 24) and bean dips, which are readily available in natural food stores and some supermarkets. You can also buy taco and enchilada sauces which are low in fat, but commercial mole sauce is usually pretty high in fat. You can make some of your own (p. 134) and freeze it. If you don't have time to make any of the "sour creams" in this book, check your health food store for low-fat, vegan commercial versions.

tostadas

Tostadas consist of flat, crisp corn tortillas with beans and salad (and sometimes other toppings and condiments) on top. Put everything out on the table, and let each diner design their own tostada. Eat with a knife and fork!

Crisp up corn tortillas by dipping each one in hot water and shaking it. Arrange the tortillas, not overlapping, on cookie sheets. Bake at 500°F for 4 minutes. Turn over and bake 2 minutes more. Use right away, or cool thoroughly and store in an airtight container for up to 5 days.

Place each crisp tortilla on a plate, and pile high with goodies:

1. *Spicy Bean Dip* (p. 50), low-fat, vegetarian "refried" beans, or plain beans, roughly mashed with a fork

2. Shredded lettuce or cabbage, chopped onions and tomatoes, maybe *Marinated Tofu Cubes* (p. 30) or smoked tofu

3. Your favorite salsa with *Tofu Cream Cheeze Spread* (p. 36), *Tofu-Cashew Sour Cream* (p. 36), or *Soy-Free Sour Cream* (p. 33).

Between the beans and salad, you can add an optional layer of grilled or steam-fried vegetables, seitan, grilled portobello or crimini mushrooms, textured vegetable protein chunks or granules, tempeh, tofu (perhaps mixed with *Mole Sauce*, p. 134, barbecue sauce, or commercial enchilada sauce), some leftover stew, or anything else that sounds tasty.

For a stacked tostada, layer fillings between two crisp tortillas. Now, dig in!

quick, open-faced enchiladas

For each serving, place 2 corn tortillas on a baking sheet. Spoon on about 3 T. *Mole Sauce* (p. 134) or a commercial enchilada sauce or even a hot barbecue sauce, almost to the edges of each tortilla. Now add any favorite enchilada filling:

low-fat "refried" beans

Spicy Bean Dip (p. 50)

corn

thawed, frozen, chopped spinach (or other green), squeezed dry

Marinated Tofu Cubes (p. 30)

crumbled, cooked vegetarian burger or "sausage"

grilled or steam-fried vegetables

tofu, coated with nutritional yeast and browned in a nonstick pan

seitan or tempeh, grilled, steam-fried, or browned

grilled portobello or crimini mushrooms

textured vegetable protein chunks or granules (perhaps mixed with more of the sauce used on the tostadas, above), grilled, steam-fried, or browned

non-traditional fillings such as *Greek-Style "Spinach Pizza"* filling (p. 103)

Top with *Melty Pizza Cheeze* (p. 42)

Bake at 350°F for 10 minutes, and serve with lime or lemon wedges, salsa, more sauce, and *Tofu Sour Cream* (p. 35), *Tofu-Cashew Sour Cream* (p. 36), or *Soy-Free Sour Cream* (p. 33).

soft tacos

Put out some of the same fillings suggested for *Tostadas* (p. 119). Each diner fills a warm corn tortilla with whatever looks good, then folds it and eats it out of hand over a plate, with lots of napkins! Serve with salsa or a commercial taco sauce and *Tofu Sour Cream* (p. 35), *Tofu-Cashew Sour Cream* (p. 36), or *Soy-Free Sour Cream* (p. 33).

One of our favorite soft taco combinations is black beans and potatoes. It may sound strange, but it's an authentic combination, and it's great on tostadas and in burritos and chimichangas too. Use *Spicy Bean Dip w/ Black Beans* (p. 50), or a low-fat instant black bean dip from a box or jar, topped with *Spicy Potatoes* (p. 174), shredded lettuce or cabbage, tomato salsa, and *Tofu Sour Cream* (p. 35), *Tofu-Cashew Sour Cream* (p. 36), or *Soy-Free Sour Cream* (p. 33). Delicious!

---

chimichangas

These are similar to burritos (see above for filling suggestions), but the cook fills and heats them all in the oven to crisp up the tortilla before serving.

Preheat the oven to 500°F. To make the tortillas more pliable before filling and folding, brush both sides lightly with nondairy "milk." Place the filling in the center of each tortilla, fold in the sides, then roll up. Don't add any salad vegetables, salsa, or "sour cream" to the filling; serve them on the side.

Place the filled tortillas on a nonstick cookie sheet, and bake for 5 minutes. Brush with nondairy "milk," and bake 3-5 minutes more, or until golden brown.

quesadillas

Originally, these were little corn turnovers with a cheese filling, but now a quesadilla is a corn or wheat tortilla, folded over and grilled, baked, or pan-fried with almost any kind of filling. Since they are not heavily filled, they make a great light meal or snack.

For each quesadilla, spread half of a corn or wheat tortilla with *Spicy Bean Dip* (p. 50), mashed beans, or commercial, low-fat vegetarian "refried" beans. If you like, add some crumbled *Marinated Tofu Cubes* (p. 30), or *Melty Pizza Cheeze* (p. 42). You can also add small amounts of any of the following:
other suggested tortilla wrap fillings
canned green or jalapeño chiles
soaked, dried tomatoes (p. 46)
chopped cilantro
rinsed, marinated artichokes
green onions
leftover *Spicy Potatoes* (p. 174)
sliced papaya
pickled vegetables
Fold the other half of the tortilla over this, and bake on cookie sheets at 500°F for 5-7 minutes until crispy. You can also grill them over hot coals, or pan-fry them in a hot, dry, nonstick or cast iron skillet until crispy on both sides. Serve with *Tofu Sour Cream* (p. 35), *Tofu-Cashew Sour Cream* (p. 36), or *Soy-Free Sour Cream* (p. 33) and your favorite salsa or taco sauce.

---

burritos

Each diner spreads mashed, cooked beans, *Spicy Bean Dip* (p. 50), or commercial, low-fat "refried" beans in the middle of a warm flour tortilla. Add any of the fillings for *Tostadas, Enchiladas,* or *Soft Tacos,* which have been put out on the table in serving dishes. Leftover rice and grain dishes are a nice addition to burritos. Fold up the bottom of the tortilla to catch drips, then wrap the sides over, and eat out of hand, with a plate and lots of napkins for drips that escape!

fajita filling

Makes enough for 8 tortillas
(soy-free)

1 lb. seitan, or ¾ lb. portobello or crimini mushrooms, cut into thin strips

1 large onion, thinly sliced

1 large red or green bell pepper, seeded and cut into strips

2 roma tomatoes, diced, or 1 c. canned diced tomatoes, drained

1-2 T. minced canned or pickled jalapeños

2-3 cloves garlic, minced

2 tsp. ground cumin

3 T. lime or lemon juice

½ c. cold vegetarian broth, dry white wine, pineapple or orange juice, or a mixture

2 tsp. cornstarch

soy sauce, to taste

OPTIONAL: 3-4 T. minced fresh cilantro

per serving: calories: 112, protein: 20 gm., fat: 0 gm., carbohydrates: 7 gm.

Originally, fajitas referred to thinly sliced, grilled skirt steak (which was marinated in a spicy lemon or lime mixture), rolled in a warm flour tortilla, and served with guacamole, salsa, and sour cream. Here is a delicious vegetarian low-fat take on the original.

Brown the seitan or mushroom strips in a large, nonstick skillet. Remove them from the pan, and set aside. Add the onion, peppers, tomatoes, jalapeños, and garlic to the hot pan, and steam-fry until the onions begin to soften. Add the seitan or mushrooms, cumin, lime or lemon juice, and broth, wine, or juice, mixed with the cornstarch, and stir until thickened. Taste the mixture—if it "needs something," add a few sprinkles of soy sauce. Add the cilantro, if using, and mix well. Serve in warm flour tortillas with salsa and *Tofu Sour Cream* (p. 35), *Tofu-Cashew Sour Cream* (p. 36), or *Soy-Free Sour Cream* (p. 33).

Variation: Instead of seitan or mushrooms, use commercial marinated or flavored tofu or tempeh, smoked tofu or *Smoky Tofu* (p. 30), flavored reconstituted textured vegetable protein chunks (p. 26), or firm, commercial, low-fat vegetarian "burgers" or "cutlets," cut into strips.

stuffed pita breads

Pita pockets are one of the most versatile of all sandwich breads. Any ordinary or exotic sandwich filling can be eaten in a pita pocket.

Felafels are traditional, but you can also use such non-traditional stuffers such as:

Oriental stir-fries and grills

fajita, burrito, taco, and enchilada fillings

hearty salads

any of the grilled foods in Chapter VII

any of the fillings for subs, heroes, gyros, tortas, peacemakers, etc. (p. 118)

burgers

chile

curry

stew

you name it!

One of my favorite ways to use pita pockets is as a crust for fillings that we would ordinarily bake, steam, or fry in bread, pastry, or noodle dough. There's no mixing, rising, rolling out, or sealing, and the baking time is minimal.

To make pita calzones, empanadas, samosas, pasties, etc., choose soft, small pitas that split easily to form pockets. Cut them in half (unless you are using mini-pitas), use a fork to ease the pocket open, and fill them quite full with your desired filling, but not so full that they split. Place them on nonstick or lightly greased cookie sheets, brush with non-dairy "milk," and bake them at 400°F for about 10-15 minutes, or until the insides are heated through. If you want the "crust" to stay soft, cover the pan loosely with foil before baking.

Italian Calzones: Use any pizza filling (see pps. 101-102).

Empanadas: Use a vegetarian piccadillo, chile, tamale pie filling, or other Latin American-style, moist and savory mixture.

Indian Samosas: Use *Kima* (p. 132), *Masala Potatoes* (p. 175), *Mattar Tofu* (p. 130), or your favorite samosa filling.

Pasties or "meat pies": Use stew-like mixtures, pot pie fillings, savory mushroom mixtures, *Upside-Down Shepherd's Pie* filling (p. 151), or a quiche filling such as *Quiche Pizza* (p. 104).

Greek-Style Pita Spinach Pies: Use the *Greek-Style "Spinach Pizza"* filling (p. 103).

Pita pockets, stuffed and heated until crisp, also make a good substitute for fried breads like Nepalese fried breads, southwestern sopapillas, or Navajo "fry-bread."

Nepalese-Style Breads: Stuff the pockets with your favorite curry mixture, and serve with chutney, *Tofu "Yogurt"* (p. 35), and other curry accompaniments.

Southwestern-Style Stuffers: Use any type of chile.

Other fillings might be used to create vegetarian Chinese steamed buns, Russian piroshki, Jamaican patties, or knishes. The fillings are usually pretty fast to mix up—it's the traditional doughs that take time to make, roll out, fill, seal, and cook. Have fun inventing your own creative, stuffed pita pockets!

hot sandwich ideas

Steamed Broccoli or Asparagus with *Melty Pizza Cheeze* (p. 42), in pita bread

Roasted or Grilled Eggplant, peppers and/or mushrooms on toast, in tortillas, or in French bread with *Melty Pizza Cheeze* (p. 42)

Seitan, or Grilled Portobello or Crimini Mushrooms (p. 113), in thin slices, hot on French bread with the juices to dip in, or hot on soft bread with *Yeast Gravy* (p. 73)

Pan-Fried or Grilled Breast of Tofu (p. 29): You can vary this sandwich by using breads such as bagels, kaiser rolls, sourdough or hard rolls, or pita instead of toast. Instead of gravy use barbecue sauce, steam-fried or grilled herbs and mushrooms, or low-fat mayonnaise flavored with chipotle chiles, or Cajun seasonings.

Vegetarian "Sausage" (p. 28), or **Burger** (p.28), sliced and seved hot on toast or a toasted bun, bagel, or English muffin with ketchup, onions, etc.

Soy *"Fish Cakes"* (p. 114), ***Teriyaki Tofu Burgers*** (p. 108), and ***Grilled Eggplant*** (p. 107), on buns or toast with all the fixings. See also some of the ideas under the listings for wrap ideas and stuffed pita bread (pps. 122).

Your Favorite Vegetarian Hot Dog with sauerkraut, chile, roasted green peppers, and pineapple chunks or other favorite trimmings.

Tofu Club Sandwich: Use grilled, extra-firm tofu, thinly sliced and soaked in teriyaki sauce (commercial or p. 108), browned in a nonstick pan or grilled. Spread toasted bread or hamburger buns with *Low-Fat Mayonnaise* (p. 32), or *Tofu Mayonnaise* (p. 31), and sprinkle with soy bacon chips. Top with lettuce, tomato, and sprouts, etc.

Quesadillas (p. 120)

Steam-Fried Mushrooms on Toast: Add a sauce, such as gravy or *Golden Cheeze Sauce* (p. 72).

"melts"

You can turn almost any sandwich into a "melt." Just top your open-faced sandwich with *Melty Pizza Cheeze* (p. 42). Heat the sandwich under a broiler until bubbly, or grill a closed sandwich in a nonstick sandwich griddle or griller.

cold sandwich fillings

Beans: Use anything from chilled, vegetarian Boston baked beans to Mexican-style *Spicy Bean Dip* (p. 50). Cold chile on a hard roll is delicious! Or try *Hummus* (p. 51) with sliced vegetables on anything from pita bread to a kaiser bun. Cold bean loaves and bean patties also make excellent sandwich fillings.

For a simple, but tasty, bean filling, coarsely mash drained, canned chick-peas. Mix with *Low-Fat Mayonnaise* (p. 32) or *Tofu Mayonnaise* (p. 31), and chopped green onions and celery. Season to taste.

Vegetables:
green onions
parsley and other herbs
lettuce and other greens
coleslaw and other prepared salads that
    hold well
sauerkraut
pickled Italian vegetables
Oriental pickles
shredded carrots
steamed or canned asparagus, etc.
Grilled Eggplant (p. 107)
marinated artichokes, well rinsed
tomatoes (try a sprinkle of soy bacon
    chips for a veggie BLT!)
soaked dried tomatoes (p. 46)
raw or roasted peppers (p. 44)
cold, grilled or steam-fried mushrooms,
    especially brown ones, such as
    portobellos (p. 113)
sprouts
cucumbers
sweet onions

Spreads:
Hummus (p. 51)
Dips (pps. 47-53), plain, flavored, or
    low-fat
Tofu Mayonnaise (p. 31)
Russian Dressing (p. 33)
Tofu Cream Cheeze Spread (p. 36)
Soy-Free Cream Cheeze (p. 38)
Tofu-Miso Pâté (p. 49)
a drizzle of fat-free vinaigrette

Fruit:

And how about some fruit for a change? A slice of apple for crunch, or a slice of pineapple or exotic mango can change an everyday sandwich into a gourmet treat.

Storing Cold Sandwiches:

If you won't be eating the sandwich soon, pack the vegetables in a separate container, and stuff the sandwich right before eating.

Meat, Dairy, and Egg Substitutes:

seitan slices

commercial smoked tofu

cold *Pan-Fried Smoky Tofu* or *Breast of Tofu* slices (pps. 29-30), or commercial chicken substitutes, sliced or chopped and mixed with mayonnaise

cold cooked vegetarian "meat loaf," "meatball," "burger," or "sausage"

commercial vegetarian "deli slices," "ham," "back bacon," "pepperoni," etc.

tofu or lentil patties, burgers, loaves, and balls

marinated tempeh

Tofu Cream Cheeze (p. 36)

Soy-Free Cream Cheeze (p. 38)

Tofu-Miso Pâté (p. 49)

Melty Pizza Cheese (p. 42)

Eggless "Egg Salad" (p. 126)

eggless "egg salad"

Makes 6 (½ cup) servings

2 (10.5 oz.) boxes extra-firm, reduced fat SILKEN tofu, drained
½ c. *Low-Fat Mayonnaise* (p. 32) or *Tofu Mayonnaise* (p. 31)
2 green onions, chopped
1 stalk celery, minced
2 T. nutritional yeast flakes
2 tsp. dry dillweed
2 tsp. turmeric
1½ tsp. prepared mustard
1 clove garlic, crushed, or ¼ tsp. garlic granules
paprika, salt, and pepper, to taste
OPTIONAL: 2 T. minced dill pickle
½ small green or red pepper, seeded and chopped

per serving: calories: 136, protein: 12 gm., fat: 7 gm., carbohydrates: 7 gm.

This is delicious not only on sandwiches, but on crackers and celery sticks.

Crumble the tofu into a bowl, and mash coarsely with a fork. Mix in the remaining ingredients; cover and refrigerate.

mock tuna salad

Makes 9 (½ cup) servings
(can be soy free)

**2 (15 oz.) cans chick-peas, drained
(3 c. cooked)**
**¾ c. *Low-Fat Mayonnaise* (p. 32) or
Tofu Mayonnaise (p. 31)**
⅔ c. minced celery
**⅓ c. minced dill pickle (or add a little
dillweed if you have no pickles)**
¼ c. nutritional yeast flakes
2 green onions, chopped
2 tsp. soy sauce (or alternate, p. 13)
1 tsp. kelp powder
**½ tsp. salt, or 1 T. light soy or chick-pea
miso**
pepper, to taste

per serving: calories: 140, protein: 6 gm.,
fat: 4 gm., carbohydrates: 19 gm.

Make sure your chick-peas are not cooked to a very soft stage for this recipe—canned chick-peas are perfect.

In a medium bowl, mash the chick-peas coarsely with a fork. Mix in the remaining ingredients, using ½ c. mayonnaise at first, and then adding more as needed. (You don't want the mixture to be too "gloppy.") Cover and refrigerate. Use on sandwiches or on a bed of salad greens.

"Mock Tuna Melt": Make open-faced sandwiches on toasted bread, cover with *Melty Pizza Cheeze* (p. 42). Broil until bubbly or grill closed sandwiches on a nonstick griddle.

carrot-oat patties

Makes 10 patties
(can be soy-free)

**2 large onions, minced or coarsely
  grated**
1 c. quick oats
**1 c. fresh whole wheat bread crumbs,
  finely crumbled**
¼ c. low-fat soy flour or chick-pea flour
1 T. tahini
1 tsp. salt
**½ tsp. EACH dried thyme, crumbled sage,
  marjoram, and garlic granules**
1 c. minced or grated carrots
⅓ c. hot water
1 T. soy sauce (or alternate, p. 13)
OPTIONAL: ½ tsp. peanut butter extract

per patty: calories: 106, protein: 4 gm.,
fat: 2 gm., carbohydrates: 17 gm.

*I used to be very fond of walnut-oat burgers, a
popular recipe that originated in Seventh Day
Adventist circles, but they were quite high in
fat. These tasty patties are quite similar in flavor, but much lower in fat—and very inexpensive to make.*

A food processor makes this recipe very
easy to assemble; otherwise, you can hand-
grate the onions and carrots fairly quickly.

In a lightly greased or nonstick skillet, steam-
fry the onion until soft. In a large bowl, mix the
oats, breadcrumbs, soy flour, tahini, salt, and
seasonings. Add the steam-fried onions, minced
or grated carrots, hot water, and soy sauce.

Mix the ingredients well and form the mixture into 10 thin patties. Cook the patties on a
nonstick or lightly oiled skillet over medium-
low heat for 4-5 minutes per side, covering the
pan while cooking the first side.

Serve the patties hot with ketchup or gravy,
or in buns. They are also excellent cold.

chapter VII

flash-in-the-pan stir-fries, sautés & oven meals

This chapter is full of fast stove-top meals that can be eaten with pasta, grains, or breads (see Chapter VI). Stir-fries are a staple for most of us, but don't overlook European-style sautés, quick stews, chiles, bean pots, and curries.

If there are two of you cooking, you can easily put together a company meal of two dishes, either rice, pasta, grain or bread, a salad, and fruit or a frozen dessert, in less than half an hour!

Check Chapter I for a rundown of optional products that can make these dishes practically fly from pan to plate—chopped ginger and garlic in jars, frozen bell pepper strips or roasted red peppers in jars, and frozen stir-fry vegetables.

You will find a few oven-baked dishes in other places, such as *Quick Open-Faced Enchiladas* and other oven-crisped wraps on p. 119, and pizza and variations on p. 102.

There were a few other excellent dishes that I didn't want to leave out, but which would not fit into any other category. I decided to assemble them in this section.

The microwave oven is an optional piece of equipment, so an ordinary oven—even a toaster oven—will do for these recipes.

mattar tofu

Serves 4

¾ lb. reduced-fat, firm tofu, cut into
   ½" cubes
2 T. grated fresh gingerroot, or 1 tsp.
   powdered ginger
1 T. chopped fresh garlic
1 medium onion, minced
1 T. garam masala or curry powder
1 tsp. salt
1 tsp. turmeric
1 tsp. ground coriander
pinch cayenne
1 (14 oz.) can diced tomatoes with juice
1½ c. frozen baby peas (petit pois)
1 tsp. liquid sweetener, sugar, or
   alternate

per serving: calories: 175, protein: 13 gm.,
fat: 4 gm., carbohydrates: 22 gm.

One of the best-loved Indian restaurant dishes is mattar panir, a tomato-flavored mixture of green peas and cubes of fresh cheese. Firm tofu makes an excellent substitute for the cheese. Serve this with rice for a complete meal.

Dry-fry the tofu cubes in a large, nonstick skillet over high heat until they are golden on two sides. Remove from the pan and set aside.

Add the ginger and garlic to the hot pan, and steam-fry over high heat with a little bit of water for a minute. Add the onion and steam-fry until it is soft, about 5 minutes. Add the seasonings and ¼ c. water or broth, stirring well, then add the tomatoes, peas, tofu, and sweetener, and simmer 10 minutes. Serve over basmati or other rice.

stir-fried peas and tofu

Serves 4-6

¾ lb. reduced-fat, extra-firm tofu

1 T. EACH nutritional yeast flakes, soy sauce, and dry sherry (or non-alcoholic alternate)

1 tsp. cornstarch

1 tsp. minced fresh gingerroot

2 c. frozen baby peas (petit pois)

1 c. low-salt vegetarian broth

3 T. soy sauce

1 tsp. sugar or alternate

4 tsp. cornstarch dissolved in 2 T. cold water

per serving: calories: 154, protein: 13 gm., fat: 3 gm., carbohydrates: 18 gm.

Children enjoy this mild, Cantonese-style dish made with ingredients that you probably always have in the house.

Cut the tofu into little squares, and toss in a bowl with the 1 T. soy sauce, yeast flakes, and sherry.

Heat a medium, nonstick skillet or wok over high heat, and brown the seasoned tofu. Add the ginger, peas, broth, 3 T. soy sauce, and sugar. Simmer until the peas are just tender, then add the dissolved cornstarch. Stir over high heat until thickened, and serve with steamed rice.

spicy szechuan eggplant

Serves 4
(can be soy-free)

2 lbs. eggplant, peeled and cut into strips about ¾" thick

1 T. minced fresh garlic

2 T. minced fresh gingerroot

1 c. vegetarian broth

¼ c. chopped green onion

2 T. EACH soy sauce (or alternate, p. 13) and vinegar

1 T. dry sherry

1 T. Szechuan hot bean paste (Chinese chile bean paste)

1 tsp. sugar or alternate

2 tsp. cornstarch dissolved in 2 T. cold water

This is a truly delicious eggplant dish!

Preheat the broiler. Place the eggplant strips on nonstick or lightly greased cookie sheets. Broil 3"-4" from the heat until browned; turn over and brown the other side. The strips should be soft.

Set a large, nonstick or lightly oiled wok or skillet over high heat. (Use Chinese sesame oil, if you have it.) Add the garlic and ginger, and steam-fry for a few seconds. Add the broiled eggplant strips, broth, green onion, soy sauce, vinegar, sherry, bean paste, and sugar. Mix well and cook over high heat for 2 minutes. Stir in the dissolved cornstarch until thickened. Transfer to a serving dish, and serve with steamed rice.

per serving: calories: 84, protein: 2 gm., fat: 0 gm., carbohydrates: 19 gm.

kima
(vegetarian kashmiri "hash")

Serves 6

1½ c. textured vegetable protein
    granules
1¼ c. very hot water
2 onions, chopped
6 cloves garlic, minced, or 2 T. minced
    garlic
1" piece of fresh gingerroot, minced
½ lb. fresh mushrooms, sliced
3 c. frozen peas and carrots, thawed
    under hot tap water
1½ c. canned diced tomatoes with juice
3 T. soy sauce or mushroom soy sauce
1-2 T. curry powder or garam masala
½ tsp. salt
1½ T. lemon juice
freshly ground black pepper, to taste
OPTIONAL: ¼ tsp. cayenne

This is an easy family meal—all you need with it is rice. Use less curry powder for children, if you prefer.

Soak the textured vegetable protein in the hot water for 10 minutes.

In a large, nonstick skillet, steam-fry the onion, garlic, and ginger until the onions start to get soft. Add the mushrooms, textured vegetable protein, peas and carrots, canned tomatoes, soy sauce, curry powder, and salt. Stir well, cover, and simmer over medium heat for 15 minutes. Add the lemon juice and black pepper (and optional cayenne, if using).

NOTE: This can be used in pita bread, as a samosa filling, or served over rice.

per serving: calories: 181, protein: 16 gm.,
fat: 0 gm., carbohydrates: 28 gm.

vegetarian hash

When my late husband Wayne was first living on his own as a young man, corned beef hash was one of his staples. Hash is a real North American low-cost "comfort food," and it's easy to make a vegetarian version.

Start with two parts of chopped, leftover, boiled or baked potatoes and one part chopped seitan (or crumbled hamburger replacement, "ready-ground" savory tofu, chopped grilled portobello or crimini mushrooms, etc.). You can add some chopped onion, mushrooms, celery, garlic, and/or green pepper. Steam-fry the onion and other optional vegetables in a nonstick skillet until they begin to soften. Add the potatoes and seitan, and sprinkle with salt, pepper, and some *Vegetarian Worcestershire Sauce* (p. 77) or steak sauce. (Chopped chives are nice too.) Drizzle in a little vegetarian broth, and let it cook over medium heat until a crust forms on the bottom. Then flip it over and let the bottom get crusty. Serve with ketchup or gravy. You can add some chopped cooked or canned beets for "Red Flannel Hash." Adding leftover chopped, cooked cabbage makes it into a sort of "Bubble 'n Squeak," an English concoction.

The hash mixture can also be bound together with a little cold, leftover vegetarian gravy or white sauce and formed into little patties, which can then be browned on a nonstick skillet. You can also substitute cooked, leftover rice or other grains, white yams, or semi-cooked sunchokes for the potatoes.

mole pinto beans

Serves 6
(soy-free)

MOLE SAUCE

3 large tomatoes, cut into chunks,
   or 2 c. canned, drained tomatoes,
   or ¼ c. tomato paste and ⅔ c. water
½ c. vegetarian broth
1 green pepper, seeded and diced
3 T. unsweetened cocoa
1½ T. tahini or peanut butter
2 T. masa harina (Mexican corn tortilla
   flour)
2 T. raisins
1½ T. dark chile powder (preferably
   ancho)
3 cloves garlic, peeled
1 tsp. EACH salt and sugar or alternate
½ tsp. ground anise
¼ tsp. ground coriander
⅛ tsp. cinnamon
dash EACH of pepper and ground cloves
   or allspice
1½ c. vegetarian broth
3 (15 oz.) cans pinto beans, drained
   (4½ c. cooked)

Mole is a distinctive Mexican sauce which contains chocolate (or cocoa, in this case). Sounds odd, but it is delicious! You can buy mole mixes, but they are usually high in fat. Ours is not. And a blender makes it so easy to prepare!

Instead of the traditional turkey or chicken, I serve it with creamy pinto beans. Eat it with salad and rice, soft, fresh Polenta (Masa Version, p. 170) or tortillas, or use as a filling for enchiladas.

In a blender, mix all of the ingredients EXCEPT the last 1½ c. of broth and the beans. Blend until very smooth. Add the remaining broth and blend again. Pour the sauce over the beans in a nonstick pot or skillet, cover, and simmer for 15-20 minutes.

Variation: Mole sauce (simmered first for 15-20 minutes) can also be served over *Pan-Fried Breast of Tofu* (p. 29), or browned seitan, tempeh, reconstituted textured vegetable protein chunks (p. 26), or your favorite cooked vegetarian "cutlet."

per serving: calories: 253, protein: 11 gm.,
fat: 3 gm., carbohydrates: 44 gm.

south american black bean pot

Serves 4
(soy-free)

1 large onion, minced
2 cloves garlic, minced
1 red or green bell pepper, or ½ of
    each, seeded and diced
2 tsp. ground cumin
1 tsp. dried oregano
½ tsp. dried red pepper flakes
2 (15 oz.) cans black beans, drained
    (3 c. cooked)
1 c. vegetarian broth
2 tomatoes, chopped, or 1½ c. canned
    diced tomatoes, drained
1 T. lemon juice
¼ c. fresh orange juice, or 1 T. frozen
    orange juice concentrate
1 tsp. salt, or to taste
freshly ground black pepper, to taste
OPTIONAL: 2 T. dark rum

Serve this easy, exotic bean dish over steamed rice with romaine lettuce and orange salad on the side.

In a nonstick or lightly oiled medium pot, steam-fry the onion and garlic for about 3 minutes. Add the peppers and steam-fry another 3 minutes. Add the cumin, oregano, and chile, and stir-fry 1 minute. Add the remaining ingredients.

Bring the beans to a boil, then turn down to medium and cook, uncovered, for 15 minutes. Just before serving, mash the beans slightly with a potato masher right in the pot, so that they are a bit creamy, but most of the beans are still intact.

per serving: calories: 210, protein: 11 gm.,
fat: 0 gm., carbohydrates: 40 gm.

lebanese lentils with greens

Serves 4
(soy-free)

1 medium onion, thinly sliced
2 cloves garlic, minced
2 (10 oz.) pkgs. cleaned, fresh spinach
leaves, or 2 (10 oz.) pkgs. frozen,
whole leaf spinach, thawed under
hot running water
2 (15 oz.) cans brown lentils, drained
(3 c. cooked)
½ c. vegetarian broth
½ tsp. salt, or to taste
1 tsp. ground cumin
freshly ground black pepper

per serving: calories: 228, protein: 15 gm.,
fat: 0 gm., carbohydrates: 41 gm.

This Middle Eastern dish is so simple, yet it remains one of my favorites. Serve it with steamed rice.

In a large, nonstick or lightly oiled pot, steam-fry the onion and garlic until the onion starts to soften. Meanwhile, thaw the frozen spinach, if you are using it, and cut either the fresh or frozen spinach into 1" pieces.

Add the lentils, spinach, broth, and seasonings. Stir well, cover, and simmer for 10-15 minutes. Taste for salt and pepper, and serve over rice.

tempeh paprikash

Serves 4-6
(can be soy-free)

1 lb. uncooked linguine or fettuccine,
    broken in half
2 medium onions, minced
1 green pepper, seeded and diced
2 T. Hungarian paprika
1 tsp. sugar or alternate
1 lb. frozen tempeh, cut into ½" cubes
2 (28 oz.) cans diced tomatoes, drained
    well
salt, to taste
1 c. *Tofu Sour Cream* (p. 35), or
    Soy-Free Sour Cream (p. 33), or
    a mixture of ⅔ (10.5 oz.) box
    reduced-fat, extra-firm SILKEN tofu,
    2 T. lemon juice, and ⅛ tsp. EACH
    sugar and salt

per serving: calories: 565, protein: 35 gm.,
fat: 11 gm., carbohydrates: 81 gm.

*This delicious Hungarian-style dish makes a
wonderful spur-of-the-moment company meal.
Accompany it with cooked linguine or fettuccine (in place of the traditional egg noodles),
cucumber salad, and steamed, frozen whole
small green beans or spinach. I like to use mild
tasting mixed-grain tempeh.*

Put a large pot of salted water on to boil for
the pasta.

In a large, nonstick skillet, steam-fry the
onion, tempeh, and pepper until the onion and
tempeh begin to brown (about 5 minutes). Add
the paprika and sugar, and stir well.

Add the tomatoes, cover, and simmer over
medium heat for 15 minutes. In the meantime,
boil the pasta and, if you have no "sour cream"
on hand, blend the tofu, lemon juice, sugar,
and salt in the food processor or with a hand
blender until it is VERY smooth.

Lower the heat and add the "sour cream" to
the tempeh mixture, stirring gently over low
heat. Taste for salt and pepper. Serve over the
hot pasta.

quick seitan or mushroom stroganoff

Serves 4-6
(can be soy-free)

1 large onion, thinly sliced
½ lb. white button mushrooms, sliced
2 c. slivered seitan or grilled brown
   mushrooms
2 c. boiling water
1 (1 oz.) packet vegetarian dried onion
   soup mix
3 T. dry sherry plus 3 T. water, or
   ⅓ c. dry white wine (or non-
   alcoholic alternative)
2 T. tomato paste
1 tsp. dry mustard
¾ c. *Tofu Sour Cream* (p. 35), *Tofu-
   Cashew Sour Cream* (p. 36), or
   Soy-Free Sour Cream (p. 33), or
   a mixture of ½ (10.5 oz.) box
   reduced-fat, extra-firm SILKEN tofu,
   1½ T. lemon juice, ¼ tsp. sugar, and
   ⅛ tsp. salt

per serving: calories: 159, protein: 22 gm.,
fat: 2 gm., carbohydrates: 10 gm.

Serve this delicious "meaty" stroganoff over hot pasta, rice, or mashed potatoes. (Start cooking these first, because the stroganoff is very quickly made.) Serve with a salad on the side.

In a large, nonstick skillet, steam-fry the onion and white mushrooms until the onion starts to soften. Add the seitan or grilled brown mushroom slivers, and stir-fry for a few minutes. Add the tomato paste along with the wine.

Dissolve the soup mix in the boiling water, and add to the pan with the wine and mustard. Simmer over medium-low heat for 5 minutes.

In the meantime, if you have no "sour cream" on hand, blend the tofu, lemon juice, salt, and sugar in a food processor or blender until VERY smooth.

Add the "sour cream" to the pan over low heat, stirring gently until heated through. Serve immediately.

Variation: Instead of seitan or mushrooms, you can use slices of firm vegetarian "burger" or marinated firm tofu.

For extra flavor, add the tomato paste to the onion and mushrooms, and stir over medium heat until the paste starts to brown. Then add the seitan or mushroom slivers.

mushrooms marengo

Serves 6
(soy-free)

2 large onions, coarsely diced
1½ lbs. whole, white or brown button
    mushrooms
1 c. vegetarian broth
¾ c. dry white wine (or non-alcoholic
    alternative)
1½ c. canned diced tomatoes, drained
1 T. EACH tomato paste and soy sauce (or
    alternate, p. 13)
1 bay leaf
½ tsp. dried thyme
1 clove garlic, crushed
1 T. potato starch dissolved in 1 T. cold
    water
salt and pepper, to taste
2 T. chopped fresh parsley

per serving: calories: 160, protein: 3 gm.,
fat: 0 gm., carbohydrates: 14 gm.

This is a vegetarian version of a classic French chicken stew. Serve it over linguine, fettuccine, mashed potatoes, rice, or polenta.

In a large, nonstick pot over high heat, steam-fry the onions until they begin to soften. Add the mushrooms and brown slightly. Add the tomato paste and stir over medium-low heat until it starts to brown. Add the tomatoes, broth, wine, soy sauce, bay leaf, thyme, and garlic. Bring to a boil, then turn down, partially cover, and simmer for 15 minutes. Stir in the dissolved potato starch, and stir until thickened. (Potato starch does not have to boil.) Add the parsley and taste for salt and pepper.

Variation: Add 1 (10 oz.) package of frozen artichoke hearts, or 1 (14 oz.) can artichoke hearts, drained and quartered.

vegetarian sukiyaki

Serves 4

SAUCE
¼ c. Japanese soy sauce or tamari
¼ c. sugar or alternate
½ c. water
2 T. dry sherry or mirin

SUKIYAKI INGREDIENTS
1 lb. reduced-fat, medium-firm tofu
OPTIONAL: **½ lb. seitan, thinly sliced**
**8-16 large shiitake mushrooms, cut in
    half, or brown mushrooms, thickly
    sliced**
**1 (10 oz.) pkg. fresh spinach leaves,
    well washed and sliced 1" thick**
**1 (8 oz.) can sliced bamboo shoots,
    rinsed and drained**
**1 bunch green onions, cut into
    2" lengths, or 1 large white onion,
    sliced**
**¼ lb. dried shirataki noodles, Oriental
    rice vermicelli, or bean thread
    (cellophane) noodles, soaked in
    warm water for 15 minutes, or 2 c.
    fresh bean sprouts**

If you have a large electric skillet, you can cook this at the table in true Japanese style.

Have all of the ingredients arranged in piles on a platter when you begin to cook.

Mix all the sauce ingredients in a small saucepan, and cook over medium-low heat while you prepare the other ingredients.

Heat a large, nonstick skillet or electric skillet. Cut the block of tofu in half horizontally, and brown the halves on both sides in the hot pan. Remove from the pan and slice the pieces about ½" thick.

Place the sliced tofu, seitan, if using, mushrooms, spinach, and bamboo shoots (and the white onion, if you are using it instead of the green onions) in separate piles in the hot pan, and pour the sauce over it all. When the sauce is bubbling and the spinach begins to wilt, turn everything over, not mixing it. Make room for the green onions and soaked noodles, and cook for a few more minutes, until the spinach and mushrooms are cooked and everything is hot. Serve immediately with steamed rice.

per serving: calories: 634, protein: 23 gm., fat: 6 gm., carbohydrates: 113 gm.

mapo doufu

Serves 4-6

**1 c. dried textured vegetable protein
granules soaked 5 minutes in ⅞ c.
hot tap water**

2 tsp. dry sherry

2 tsp. soy sauce

**2 tsp. hoisin sauce, or 1 tsp. EACH dark
miso and liquid sweetener**

2 tsp. minced garlic

4 tsp. minced fresh gingerroot

**4 tsp. Szechuan hot bean paste or
Chinese chile bean paste, or 2-4
dried hot red peppers, crumbled**

**1 lb. reduced-fat, medium-firm tofu, cut
into ½" cubes and placed in a
colander to drain**

1½ c. water

¼ c. soy sauce

4 green onions, thinly sliced

**4 T. cornstarch mixed with 4 T. cold
water**

per serving: calories: 183, protein: 20 gm.,
fat: 4 gm., carbohydrates: 17 gm.

*This is another very easy, family-style, spicy
Chinese dish which can be served with rice or
noodles and steamed or stir-fried vegetables. It
can also be served as part of a larger Chinese
meal. Instead of the traditional ground pork,
we use textured vegetable protein.*

Mix the soaked textured vegetable protein
with the sherry, the 2 tsp. soy sauce, and the
hoisin sauce, and set aside.

Heat a large, lightly oiled or nonstick skillet
or wok over high heat. Add the garlic and ginger, and steam-fry briefly. Add the textured vegetable protein mixture, and stir-fry for 2 minutes.
Add the hot bean paste, tofu, water, and the
¼ c. soy sauce. Simmer for 3 minutes.

Add the green onions and cornstarch mixture, and stir over high heat until thick and
bubbly. Serve immediately.

quick sukiyaki noodles

Serves 4
(can be soy-free)

4 c. cooked vermicelli, spaghettini, soba, or other thin pasta (½ lb. uncooked)*

½ c. low-salt vegetarian broth

½ c. Japanese soy sauce (or alternate, p. 13)

¼ c. dry sherry (or non-alcoholic alternative)

2 T. sugar or alternate

1 bunch green onions, cut into 1" lengths

½ lb. mushrooms, sliced

1 T. cornstarch

1 lb. Chinese celery cabbage (bok choy), cut in strips, or 8 oz. savoy cabbage, thinly sliced

1 (10 oz.) pkg. fresh spinach leaves, well washed and trimmed

OPTIONAL: 1 (10.5 oz.) box reduced-fat, extra-firm SILKEN tofu, or ½ lb. reduced-fat, medium-firm tofu or seitan, thinly sliced

toasted sesame seeds to sprinkle on top

per serving: calories: 111, protein: 5 gm., fat: 0 gm., carbohydrates: 17 gm.

This is an easy Americanized version of a Japanese dish (see p. 140 for a more authentic version). It's also a good way to use up that leftover pasta from last night.

If using uncooked pasta, put on a large pot of water to boil. Add the pasta to the boiling water, stirring well.

Stir together the broth, soy sauce, sherry, and sugar in a measuring cup.

In a very hot, lightly greased or nonstick skillet or wok, steam-fry the green onions for 2-3 minutes. Add the mushrooms and stir-fry for 1 minute. Add ½ c. of the soy sauce mixture to the pan, along with the Chinese celery cabbage or savoy cabbage. Stir over high heat 1 minute, then cover and cook for 1 more minute (2 minutes for savoy cabbage).

Check the pasta; when al dente (tender, but not soft), drain into a colander and rinse with cold water. Mix the cornstarch into the remaining soy sauce mixture. Add to the pan and stir over high heat until it begins to thicken.

Add the spinach and cooked pasta. Cover and cook over medium heat for about 3 minutes, stirring once or twice. When the spinach wilts and the noodles are hot, toss well and serve immediately.

*NOTE: You can also use ½ lb. Asian vermicelli, soaked in warm water for 15 minutes before being added to the pan with the spinach. Do not boil.

142

szechuan bean curd (tofu)

Serves 6

1½ lbs. reduced-fat, medium-firm tofu, cut into ½" cubes

6 large, brown cultivated or shiitake mushrooms, chopped*

6 green onions, cut into short lengths

¼ c. dry sherry (or non-alcoholic alternative)

2 T. Szechuan hot bean paste (Chinese chile bean paste)

2 T. soy sauce

2 tsp. Chinese black bean sauce

2 tsp. cornstarch dissolved in 2 T. cold water

OPTIONAL: roasted ground Szechuan pepper, to taste

per serving: calories: 167, protein: 15 gm., fat: 5 gm., carbohydrates: 13 gm.

*If you have time, you can use 6 dried Chinese mushrooms, reconstituted as on p. 46, instead of fresh mushrooms. After soaking, remove the stems and discard them. Use 2 T. of the soaking water to dissolve the cornstarch.

If you like hot foods, you'll love this simple, super-fast Chinese dish. Serve with rice or noodles and steamed or stir-fried vegetables, or as part of a larger Chinese meal.

Szechuan peppercorns have a distinctive flavor. Look for them in health food stores, Oriental grocery stores, or the Chinese food section of large supermarkets. Toast them in a hot, dry skillet until they are aromatic, then grind in a blender or spice grinder, and store in an airtight container.

Steam-fry the mushrooms and onions in a hot, medium, lightly oiled or nonstick skillet or wok for a couple of minutes.

Add the tofu cubes and a mixture of the sherry, soy sauce, chile paste, and black bean sauce. Stir over high heat for 3-4 minutes. Add the dissolved cornstarch and stir to thicken. Sprinkle with the Szechuan pepper, if you have it, and serve with rice or hot wheat tortillas.

chinese "beef" and broccoli in vegetarian "oyster" sauce

Serves 4-6
(can be soy-free)

2 c. seitan, grilled brown mushrooms, or reconstituted textured vegetable protein chunks (p. 26), cut into slivers

2 T. soy sauce (or alternate, p. 13)

1 tsp. cornstarch

1 thin slice gingerroot, minced

1 large clove garlic, minced or crushed

1 large onion, cut into 6 wedges, layers separated

1 bunch broccoli, stalk peeled and cut into small pieces

3-4 T. *Vegetarian "Oyster" Sauce* (p. 145)

pinch EACH of salt and sugar

½ c. cold water or light vegetarian broth mixed with a scant T. cornstarch.

per serving: calories: 148, protein: 21 gm., fat: 1 gm., carbohydrates: 14 gm.

This was one of the first Chinese dishes that I learned to make years ago from a Vancouver friend, Benjamin Lee. Vegetarian "oyster" sauce, made from mushrooms, can be purchased in many Oriental grocery stores—or you can make your own (p. 145).

Mix the seitan slivers (or alternate) with the soy sauce and 1 tsp. cornstarch. Heat a non-stick wok or large skillet over high heat. Add the garlic, ginger, and seitan. Steam-fry until the seitan is browned. Remove from the pan and set aside. Add the broccoli and onion to the pan, and add 2 T. water. Cover and steam for 2-3 minutes, or until the broccoli is just crisp-tender. (Add a little more water if necessary.) Add the seitan or alternate back to the pan, along with the remaining ingredients. Stir until the sauce is thickened, and serve with steamed rice.

Szechuan "Beef" and Broccoli Stir-Fry: Use dark soy sauce, if possible. Omit the minced ginger and use 6 cloves of garlic. If you like, add a seeded red bell pepper, cut into squares, for color. Omit the "oyster" sauce and salt, and use instead 1 T. vinegar and 1 T. Szechuan hot bean paste (Chinese chile bean paste). Add ½ T. sugar and 1 c. light vegetarian broth.

Broccoli and "Beef" in Black Bean Sauce: Increase the ginger to 1 tsp. and the garlic to 2 tsp. Use bottled Chinese black bean sauce (or the homemade, soy-free version on p. 112) instead of the "oyster" sauce.

vegetarian "oyster" sauce

Makes ½ cup (4 servings)
(can be soy-free)

1 Hugli mushroom broth cube
½ c. boiling water
2 T. Chinese brown bean sauce or dark
**   soy or chick-pea miso**
1 generous T. Sucanat or brown sugar
1 tsp. cornstarch dissolved in 1 tsp. cold
**   water**

per serving: calories: 29, protein: 1 gm., fat: 0 gm., carbohydrates: 5 gm.

Chinese oyster sauce is great for stir-fries. You can find a commercial vegetarian version, made with mushrooms, in some Oriental groceries. If you can't buy it, though, it's easy to make.

Dissolve the broth cube in the boiling water. Mix with the brown bean sauce and sugar in a small saucepan, and heat to boiling. Add the dissolved cornstarch and stir until thickened. Cool and store in a covered jar in the refrigerator.

cutlets dijon

Serves 4
(can be soy-free)

4 c. sliced fresh mushrooms

⅔ c. dry sherry or dry vermouth (or non-alcoholic alternative)

½ c. reduced-fat soy or other non-dairy "milk," blended smooth with ½ c. crumbled, reduced-fat, medium-firm tofu

Use one of the following for the cutlets:
12-16 slices *Pan-Fried Breast of Tofu* (p. 28), or 8 thin seitan patties or cutlets, or 2 c. flavored reconstituted textured vegetable protein chunks

¼ c. Dijon mustard

1 T. chicken-style vegetarian broth powder

2 tsp. lemon juice

salt, to taste

dash EACH freshly ground pepper and nutmeg

per serving: calories: 242, protein: 25 gm., fat: 4 gm., carbohydrates: 18 gm.

This elegant dish can be made with Pan-Fried Breast of Tofu *(p. 28); mildly-flavored seitan cutlets; your favorite "chicken-style" commercial vegetarian "burger," "cutlet," or "fillet"; mildly flavored, commercial baked savory tofu; reconstituted textured vegetable protein chunks (p. 26); or commercial marinated tempeh "grills."*

In a large, nonstick skillet over high heat, steam-fry the mushrooms until browned. Add the wine and scrape up all the brown residue. Stir in the blended "milk" mixture, mustard, and seasonings.

Stir medium-high heat for a few minutes, taste for salt, then keep warm over very low heat while you brown the "cutlets" by sautéing in a nonstick pan or by grilling. Serve the sauce over the hot "cutlets," or add browned textured soy protein chunks directly to the reconstituted sauce in the pan. Serve immediately with rice or other grain, pasta, or potatoes.

To Make Soy-Free: Blend the "milk" with ½ c. cooked short grain brown rice instead of tofu.

cacciatore cutlets

Serves 4-6
(can be soy-free)

Use one of the following for the cutlets:
    12-16 slices *Pan-Fried Breast of Tofu*
    (p. 28), or 8 thin seitan patties or
    cutlets, or 2 c. flavored reconstituted
    textured vegetable protein chunks

¾-1 lb. linguine or fettuccine, broken up

CACCIATORE SAUCE
½ lb. fresh mushrooms (any variety),
    sliced
1 onion, sliced
1 green pepper, seeded and sliced
2 cloves garlic, minced or crushed
1 (28 oz.) can diced tomatoes, drained
¾ c. dry white or red wine, dry sherry,
    or dry white vermouth, or use ¾ c.
    juice from the canned tomatoes and
    1 T. balsamic vinegar
1 tsp. salt
½ tsp. sugar or alternate
½ tsp. EACH dried rosemary and thyme
    (or ½ T. fresh)
OPTIONAL: **a few drops of liquid smoke**
        1 tsp. potato starch dissolved
            in 1 T. cold water

Brown the cutlets in a nonstick skillet or on a grill. Cook the pasta. In a large, nonstick skillet, steam-fry the mushrooms, onion, green pepper, and garlic until tender. Add the remaining ingredients and the "cutlets." Cook the sauce down a bit. If you have to, thicken with the potato starch; do not boil. Taste for seasoning and serve over the pasta.

per serving: calories: 508, protein: 35 gm.,
fat: 3 gm., carbohydrates: 71 gm.

vegetarian cutlets canzanese

Serves 4
(can be soy-free)

Use one of the following for the cutlets:
¾ lb. reduced-fat, extra-firm tofu
1 (8 oz.) package tempeh, cut into
16 thin slices
2 cups reconstituted, flavored
textured vegetable protein
chunks (p. 26)
12 oz. lightly flavored seitan or
chicken-flavored seitan cutlets

OPTIONAL: **2 T. light soy sauce**
(or alternate, p. 13)
OPTIONAL: **¼ c. nutritional yeast flakes**
¼ lb. fresh mushrooms, sliced
½ c. dry white wine (or non-alcoholic
alternative)
½ c. vegetarian broth
8 cloves garlic, minced or crushed
3 whole fresh sage leaves
2 bay leaves
1 tsp. dried rosemary, or 1 T. fresh,
chopped
freshly ground black pepper, to taste
pinch of dried red hot pepper flakes
8 lemon wedges for garnish
OPTIONAL: **1 T. soy bacon chips, soaked**
in ¼ c. hot water and drained,
or ¼ c. minced vegetarian "ham" or
"back bacon"

This is delicious over steamed rice. If you have some Breast of Tofu *(p. 29) marinating, you can just brown that in a nonstick pan instead of preparing the tofu in the manner below.*

If using the tofu slices, place them in a shallow baking pan, and cover with the soy sauce. (It will be absorbed.) Dredge the slices in the nutritional yeast flakes.

If using tempeh, simmer it for 5 minutes in vegetarian broth.

Brown the cutlets of your choice on all sides in a nonstick pan. Add the mushrooms to the hot pan, and brown briefly. Add the remaining ingredients and simmer, uncovered, over medium heat for about 10-15 minutes, or until the sauce is reduced somewhat. Serve with lemon wedges over rice.

per serving: calories: 175, protein: 15 gm., fat: 4 gm., carbohydrates: 12 gm.

Variation: This is similar to the *Vegetarian Cutlets Canzanese*, at left, but more flexible—you can make it with Italian, French, or Greek-style seasoning, depending upon the herbs, vegetables, and liquids you use. I like it with rice, but you can serve it with polenta, noodles, or any grain you prefer.

¼-½ lb. mushrooms (any kind), sliced
½ onion, chopped
4-8 cloves garlic, minced or crushed
¼ c. chopped fresh herbs of choice, or 1 T. dried (oregano, basil, tarragon, sage, savory, rosemary, parsley, etc.)
salt and freshly ground pepper, to taste
½ c. vegetarian broth
½ c. dry white wine
OPTIONAL: 1 tsp. potato starch dissolved in 1 T. cold water for thickening, if necessary

OPTIONAL: Use any or all of the following:
green and/or red pepper, seeded and sliced
juice and slivered rind of ½ lemon
1 c. canned quartered artichoke hearts, drained
2 T. sliced dried tomatoes
1 T. soy bacon chips
1 or 2 stalks celery, sliced

Brown the cutlets of your choice, then add the mushrooms, onion, garlic, herbs of your choice, and optional ingredients. Steam-fry for a few minutes, then add the broth and wine, and simmer over medium heat, uncovered, for 10-15 minutes, or until reduced somewhat. Thicken with the optional starch, if necessary. Serve over rice, noodles, polenta, etc.

Cutlets with 20 Cloves of Garlic: Use basil, parsley, and oregano or tarragon for the herbs. Add 20 whole, peeled cloves of garlic. You can use cognac instead of wine, if you like. The garlic can be mashed and spread on French bread toast. Delicious!

scallopine vegetariana

Serves 4
(can be soy-free)

**2 c. reconstituted, flavored textured
vegetable protein chunks (p. 26)**
***Seasoned Coating Mix* (p. 45) or plain
flour**
olive oil cooking spray
3 cloves garlic, minced
**1 T. minced fresh rosemary, or 1 tsp.
dried**
**½ c. dry white wine (or non-alcoholic
alternative)**
**1 c. vegetarian broth (preferably
chicken-style)**
**1 c. canned diced tomatoes, drained, or
diced fresh tomatoes**
grated zest of 1 lemon
1-2 T. fresh lemon juice
salt and freshly ground pepper, to taste

per serving: calories: 183, protein: 21 gm.,
fat: 0 gm., carbohydrates: 16 gm.

Scallopine is the term used for very thin Italian-style cutlets ("scallops" or "medallions"). Textured vegetable protein chunks work very well in this type of quick dish. The chunks can be reconstituted and flavored in large amounts, then frozen in 2-cup containers for later use (p. 26).

Dredge the chunks in the flour. Mist a heavy, nonstick skillet with the cooking spray, and heat on high heat. Brown the chunks, add the garlic and rosemary, and stir-fry for a minute. Add the wine and stir until it thickens a bit.

Add the broth, tomatoes, and lemon zest. Keep stirring over high heat until a nice sauce forms. Add the lemon juice and salt and pepper to taste. Serve immediately with rice, pasta, polenta, or potatoes.

To Make Soy-Free: Substitute very thin seitan cutlets, prepared the same way.

hawaiian sticky tofu

Serves 4

**¾ lb. reduced-fat, extra-firm tofu, cut
into 16 slices**

SAUCE
6 T. Japanese soy sauce
2 green onions
1 large clove garlic, peeled
1 tsp. cornstarch
¾ tsp. agar powder, or 1½ T. agar flakes
½ c. plus 2 T. hot water
¼-⅓ c. liquid sweetener
1½ tsp. chicken-style broth powder
**½ tsp. EACH powdered ginger and
ground mustard powder**
**1 (14-19 oz.) can pineapple chunks,
drained**
**1 large green or red bell pepper (or
½ of each), seeded and cut into
squares**

per serving: calories: 251, protein: 13 gm.,
fat: 4 gm., carbohydrates: 40 gm.

Serve this with steamed rice and raw vegetables for a kid-pleasing meal. Leftovers are delicious cold!

Preheat the oven to 500°F. Quickly fry the tofu slices in a nonstick pan until browned on both sides. Place in one layer in a nonstick or lightly oiled 9" x 13" baking pan.

Place the soy sauce, green onion, garlic, cornstarch, and agar in a blender, and combine well. Add the remaining ingredients EXCEPT the pineapple and green pepper. Mix well, then pour into a saucepan, and stir over high heat until it boils. Stir and continue to simmer for about 1 minute. Add the pineapple and green pepper, then pour over the tofu in the pan. Bake for 15 minutes.

quick baked potatoes with toppers

Baked potatoes for a quick meal? Well, not your normal baked potatoes, I admit, but, with the help of a microwave oven or a pressure cooker, you can have baked potatoes on the table in under half an hour—even the crispy-skinned kind that I like!

We often have baked potatoes with Rich Brown Yeast Gravy *(p. 73) and/or* Tofu Sour Cream *(p. 35),* Tofu-Cashew Sour Cream *(p. 36), or* Soy-Free Sour Cream *(p. 33), chives or green onions, soy bacon chips, and some steamed veggies on the side for a simple, but satisfying, meal. Leftover potatoes can be cubed and browned in a nonstick pan the next day, or reheated in the microwave for another meal. But you can get much more inventive with a baked potato, as you will see from the list of possible toppers on p. 154.*

Scrub Russet or Yukon Gold potatoes. (Make sure they are all about the same size and shape.) Poke them in several places with a fork.

For the microwave method, line the carousel of your microwave with two layers of paper towelling. Position the potatoes like the spokes of a wheel, evenly spaced, or stick them upright in the cups of a microwave muffin pan. For 6 medium potatoes, cook on high for 10-12 minutes, depending upon the wattage of your oven. While the potatoes pre-cook in the microwave, preheat your oven or toaster oven to 500°F, and prepare your topping(s). *More or less potatoes will require more or less cooking time.*

To make a crispy skin, place the potatoes immediately in the hot oven or toaster oven, and bake for 10-15 minutes before splitting and serving.

For the Pressure-Cooker Method, place medium potatoes in the steam-basket of your pressure cooker or on a folding steamer basket, and place over several inches of water. Lock the lid in place, and bring to 15 lbs. pressure over high heat, then turn down just enough to maintain this pressure. Cook 10 minutes. In the meantime, preheat your oven or toaster oven to 500°F, and prepare your topping(s). When the 10 minutes is up, bring the pressure down quickly under cold running water, and immediately place the potatoes in your hot oven or toaster oven to crisp up for 15 minutes—then split and serve. NOTE: You can cook as many potatoes as your pressure cooker can comfortably hold—just make them all the same size.

Toppings: Besides *Rich Brown Yeast Gravy* (p. 73) and "sour cream" with the customary chives or green onions and soy bacon bits, you can use any favorite creamy sauce, salad dressing or dip, stir-fry, chile, spaghetti sauce, sloppy joe topping, or stew that you like—leftovers are excellent for this. Just plain, steamed, stir-fried, or grilled vegetables with a sauce, or just soy sauce and garlic are delicious.

Here is a list of possibilities:

Vegetable Dip (p. 48)

Classic Spinach Dip (p. 48)

Golden Cheeze Sauce, with or without steamed vegetables (p. 72) (You can also add some chopped vegetarian "ham" or "back bacon," mushrooms, etc.)

South American Black Bean Pot (p. 135)

Mole Pinto Beans (p. 134)

Mattar Tofu (p. 130)

Creamy Fresh Herb Dressing (p. 82)

Kima (p. 132)

Pomodoro Crudo (p. 94)

Fajita Filling (p. 121)

sliced seitan au jus

Tempeh Paprikash (p. 137)

Quick Seitan Stroganoff (p. 138)

Mushrooms Marengo (p. 139)

Szechuan Bean Curd (p. 143)

Cacciatore Cutlets (p. 147)

Scallopine Vegetariana (p. 150)

Upside-Down Vegetable Shepherd's Pie Filling (p. 151)

Vegetarian Cutlets Canzanese and variations (p. 148)

grilled or steam-fried vegetables

steam-fried or grilled mushrooms (p. 113)

steam-fried greens

upside-down vegetable shepherd's pie

Serves 4
(can be soy-free)

2 c. mashed potatoes

FILLING
1 carrot, peeled and finely diced
1 large onion, chopped
¼ lb. fresh mushrooms, sliced
1 green pepper, seeded and diced
Use one of the following:
    ¾ c. dry textured vegetable protein granules reconstituted with ⅔ c. very hot water and 1 T. dark soy sauce or mushroom soy sauce
    1 c. canned or cooked lentils, drained
    1 c. crumbled, low-fat vegetarian burger replacement
    1 c. ground seitan
½ c. hot water mixed with ½ T. yeast extract or dark miso
1 T. chopped fresh parsley
1 T. ketchup
½ tsp. dried thyme
black pepper, to taste
2 T. soy Parmesan (omit and use bread crumbs for soy-free version)

There's nothing more comforting than a shepherd's pie. This quick version is much tastier than its humble components suggest. If you have leftover mashed potatoes, use them in this recipe. Otherwise, use instant mashed potatoes according to the package directions. (There is an organic brand available in natural food stores.)

Preheat the oven to 400°F. Press the mashed potatoes onto the bottom and sides of a lightly oiled or nonstick 9" pie pan. Place this in the oven while it is heating.

In a large, nonstick or lightly oiled skillet, steam-fry the onion, mushrooms, and carrot until tender. Add the green pepper, vegetable protein or alternate, and remaining ingredients. Stir over high heat until most of the liquid is absorbed. Spoon into the partially cooked potato "crust," sprinkle with the soy Parmesan, and bake for 10 minutes. Serve with steamed vegetables or salad.

Variations: Try this using leftover rice or frozen, fat-free grated potatoes as the crust. You can use any kind of cooked or canned beans in place of the lentils, if you prefer. Add some cooked or defrosted corn kernels and/or peas to the filling. You can vary the seasoning to make this pie a little more exotic too. For instance, add a teaspoon of curry powder or ½ tsp. each of cumin and oregano, with a pinch of chile flakes.

per serving: calories: 184, protein: 11 gm., fat: 1 gm., carbohydrates: 29 gm.

swift & easy side dishes

More likely than not, when you're in a hurry, your side dishes are going to be pretty basic—steamed rice, couscous, noodles, *Quick-Baked Potatoes* (p. 153), bread, or toast. Vegetables will be a salad, raw vegetable dippers, or steamed or stir-fried fresh or frozen vegetables.

But if your main dish is simple (a vegetarian burger or patty or a bare-bones stir-fry), you may wish to spend your small allotment of cooking time on an interesting grain or potato dish to spark up the meal. Or the grain, vegetable, or potato dish might BE the main dish.

a few words about vegetable side dishes

Don't be apologetic about using frozen vegetables during the winter or when preparation time is at a premium. Experiment to find good-quality brands that you can depend on. (There are even organic, frozen vegetables available.) Vegetables are frozen at their peak of flavor and nutrition, so they are often more nutritious and cheaper than those bags of "fresh," cut-up vegetables that you can buy in the produce section. Since I live in Canada, I depend on frozen spinach, peas (especially baby peas or petit pois), corn (the "peaches and cream" variety is delicious), and small, whole green beans during the winter. This type of green bean (unlike the cut or julienned type) is absolutely delicious and can be purchased cheaply in bulk bags. You might even want to splurge occasionally on frozen snow peas, asparagus tips, baby limas, or artichoke hearts.

I sometimes buy frozen mixed peas and diced carrots to add to some dishes—it eliminates peeling and dicing the carrots. Carrots and other vegetables are also available sliced frozen in 2 lb. (1 kg) bags, plain or in various combinations, ready for steaming or stir-frying.

I usually use fresh carrots because they are cheaper. I use fresh broccoli and other cabbage family vegetables because they are easily available and quick to clean and cut. I also prefer fresh mushrooms.

I most often steam, braise in vegetable broth, or stir-fry the vegetables I cook. Most vegetables are delicious seasoned with a little salt, pepper, and garlic. You can use a sprinkling of toasted sesame oil for a richer flavor. Toss them with *On-the-Spot Creamy "Butter" Sauce* (p. 74). Broccoli, cauliflower, and cabbage are wonderful with *Golden Cheeze Sauce* (p. 72). Be creative with other vegetarian seasonings and sauces:

soy Parmesan

Tofu Sour Cream (p. 35), or soy-free version (p. 33)

"Hollandaise" (p. 31)

barbecue sauce

Quick Creamy Sauce (p. 75)

You can also try commercial toppings like herbal salts, chopped veggie "ham" or "back bacon," no-fat vinaigrette dressing, fresh minced gingerroot, balsamic vinegar, and Chinese sauces. Leftover vegetables can be used in soups or mixed with a creamy sauce, topped with bread crumbs, and baked.

quick spinach

If you are in a tearing hurry, just stick an unopened box of frozen whole spinach in the microwave for 7 minutes on HIGH—it serves two and tastes wonderful!

stir-frying vegetables

Don't stir-fry in hot oil, but with a bit of water or broth instead. The technique is similar to steam-frying (p. 11). Have your vegetables cut ahead of time, and arrange them by length of cooking time. It's a good idea to blanch or partially cook less tender vegetables ahead of time, plunging them into ice cold water after draining, so they remain crisp and brightly colored. (This is unnecessary if you are using frozen vegetables.) Lightly oil a large, heavy skillet or wok with about ½ teaspoon of oil. (Chinese sesame oil is a nice choice for Oriental dishes.) Heat it over high heat. Add onions and garlic, if using, and a few other vegetables, and stir-fry until they are crisp-tender. Add just enough liquid to keep them from sticking. Add your seasonings or cooking sauce, toss briefly, and serve.

quick-cooking root vegetables

To quick-cook these hard vegetables and preserve their color, flavor, and nutrition, peel and grate beets, carrots, turnips, rutabagas, parsnips, parsley root, celeriac, bulb fennel, kohlrabi, salsify, etc., alone or in combination. For about 6 c. (total) of grated vegetables, use ¼-½ c. vegetarian broth. Place the veggies and broth (and any seasonings you would like) in a nonstick wok or large skillet. Bring to a boil, turn the heat down to medium, cover, and steam for about 5 minutes until tender. Taste for salt and boil away any excess liquid that may remain. Delicious!

roasted garlic and/or onion sauce for vegetables

An absolutely delicious sauce for steamed vegetables can be made by combining about equal parts vegetarian broth and *Quick-Roasted (Caramelized) Garlic and/or Onions* (p. 44). You can just mash the roasted vegetables a little with a fork, and then mix in the broth, or you can blend them in a food processor or blender, depending on the texture you want. Cook this for a few minutes, stirring, in an uncovered nonstick pan. You can add some diced red bell pepper while it cooks, for color. Taste for salt and pepper, and toss with drained, steamed vegetables, or pour it over the top. I like this on steamed broccoli, especially with the red pepper for color contrast.

grains

The majority of the recipes in this section are rice dishes, because rice is the most universally preferred grain and goes well with so many foods. However, for those of you who would like to be adventurous and try other quick-cooking grains, such as bulgur wheat and quinoa, consult the chart on p. 159 for cooking times, amounts, and yields. Or follow the directions for pilaf variations using different grains (p. 160). I don't use either a microwave or a pressure cooker for these other quick-cooking grains, because I find that it's less fuss to just start cooking them over low heat on the stove before I start the rest of the meal. They take care of themselves in 15-25 minutes with no interference from me.

preparing quick-cooking grains				
Grain (1 Cup)	Cups Liquid	Salt (optional)	Cooking Times	Yield in Cups
Amaranth	2	½ tsp. **	20-25 minutes	2
Buckwheat	2	½ tsp.	10-12 minutes ***	2
Bulgur Wheat	2-2½	½ tsp.	20 minutes ***	3
Millet*	2½	½ tsp.	20 minutes ***	3½-4
Quinoa* (Wash well before cooking to remove a natural, strong-tasting resin.)	2	½ tsp.	12-15 minutes	3-3½

*Toast grains lightly in a dry pan before boiling. This is an important step in cooking some grains.

** Add salt after cooking.

*** Plus 10 minutes standing time

a fast way to prepare couscous

You can prepare regular couscous as quickly as the instant variety if you use this method. Toast 1⅓ c. regular couscous (whole wheat is fine) in a preheated, nonstick or lightly oiled skillet or medium saucepan over medium heat, stirring for 2 minutes. (This will keep the grains separate.) Remove from the heat and stir in 2 c. boiling vegetarian broth. Cover and let stand 10 minutes. Fluff with a fork. This comes out fluffier than using instant couscous. If you are allergic to wheat, use Lunenburg Farms RizCous.

pilaf

Serves 6-8
(soy-free)

1 large onion, chopped
1 c. chopped celery
1 c. bulgur wheat
1 c. converted or basmati rice, or quick-
**   cooking brown rice**
1 tsp. dried rosemary, crushed, or dried
**   thyme or oregano**
OPTIONAL: ½ tsp. curry powder or
**   ground coriander**
¼ c. minced fresh parsley
3½ c. vegetarian broth
salt, to taste

per serving: calories: 144, protein: 4 gm.,
fat: 0 gm., carbohydrates: 31 gm.

Pilaf is a Middle Eastern term for a flavored rice mixture. You can also make a pilaf with other grains. Try amaranth, millet, oats, or quinoa for a change. Consult the cooking chart on p. 159.

In a large, nonstick or lightly oiled saucepan with a tight fitting lid, steam-fry the onion and celery until the onion starts to soften. Add the bulgur, rice, rosemary, and curry powder, and steam-fry for a minute. Add the broth (and a bit of salt, if you prefer), bring to a boil, then turn down, cover, and cook on low for 20 minutes. Let stand for 5 minutes. Fluff with a fork before serving.

You can also use all bulgur wheat (and use 4 c. broth), or all rice (and use 3 c. broth), instead of a mixture.

Variations: Add a chopped or shredded carrot or ¼ lb. chopped mushrooms to the vegetables when you steam-fry them. Add a couple of tablespoons of roasted sesame seeds, if you like. Other additions might be:
 minced garlic
1 c. frozen, whole, small green beans,
    broken and thawed
1 c. cubed or grated summer squash
1 c. corn kernels
chopped red or green bell pepper
1 c. chopped broccoli or other vegetables or
    a mixture of vegetables
chopped apple with ½ tsp. cinnamon
You can also add bits of chopped seitan, vegetarian "sausage," or other meat replacement for a more substantial dish.

Greek-Style Pilaf: Add 4 whole cloves. You can use some white wine as part of the liquid.
Turkish Pilaf: Add some chopped green onions and dried currants or raisins. A couple of tablespoons of lemon juice (and perhaps the grated zest of a lemon) is also tasty in a pilaf.

colored and flavored rice

Check the *Pilaf* recipe on the facing page for ideas for flavored rice dishes.

In South America and South Africa, yellow rice is often served. In South America, the yellow color is usually achieved by using annatto seeds, but ½ tsp. of turmeric per cup of rice, as used in Africa, works fine. Both methods cook steam-fried onion with the rice. For the African version, add a 2" cinnamon stick and ½ c. of raisins for each cup of rice used. For the South American version, you can use vegetarian broth or water for the liquid, and add ½ c. peas, if you wish.

Orange rice is also delicious—be sure to use white rice. Use half orange juice and half vegetarian broth for the liquid, and add 1-3 tsp. of grated orange peel per cup of rice. You can also add steam-fried onion, garlic, parsley, celery, and herbs, if you like. One-half c. of raisins and/or some shredded carrot also makes a nice addition.

For green rice, add 1 c. chopped, fresh green herbs, such as parsley, cilantro, basil, dill, etc. If you wish, add a (10 oz.) pkg. of frozen, chopped spinach, thawed under hot running water in a colander, and squeezed dry, to plain rice or pilaf. You can add some minced green chiles for a Mexican-style green rice.

NOTE OF CAUTION: Do not cook brown rice in tomato juice or with other acid products (such as fruit juices, dried fruits, etc.). They harden the bran on the outside of the rice. This makes it take MUCH, much longer to cook.

quick curried rice

Serves 4-6
(can be soy-free)

4 medium onions, minced

3 stalks celery, sliced

OPTIONAL: **1 c. sliced mushrooms**

1 c. frozen peas

½ c. raisins or dried currants

1 tsp. (or more) garam masala or curry powder

4 c. cooked long grain rice (preferably brown)

½ tsp. salt

pepper, to taste

OPTIONAL: **1 c. chopped seitan, savory tofu, or other meat replacement**

1 c. canned unsweetened pineapple tidbits, drained

per serving: calories: 362, protein: 9 gm.,
fat: 5 gm., carbohydrates: 69 gm.

This versatile dish is a good way to use leftover rice, and it makes a great stuffing for squash and other vegetables too. The addition of seitan, tofu, etc., turns it into a main dish.

In a large, nonstick or lightly oiled skillet, steam-fry the onions, celery, and any optional ingredients until they soften. Add the curry powder and stir-fry for 1 minute. Add the rice and other ingredients, and steam-fry until the whole mixture is hot.

basic stove-top rice

I made mushy rice for years, until I discovered that most rice recipes call for too much liquid. I use 1½ c. liquid for every 1 c. dry rice, no matter what kind of rice or how much. I know that these proportions are not orthodox—most books tell you to use more liquid for brown rice or for long grain rice, and to use a little less water for each extra cup of rice, etc. But this formula has always worked perfectly for me. I also don't wash rice.

The only variation is that I pour long grain rice slowly into boiling water or broth (to make the grains more separate), but I start short grain rice in cold water.

Salt is optional. Asian cooks usually don't use it, so I just put in a pinch (large or small, depending upon the size of the pot) when preparing non-Oriental recipes. Some recipes call for 1 tsp. salt for a cup of rice, but I would certainly never use more than ¼-½ tsp. per cup. For very separate grains of long grain white rice, add 1 tsp. of lemon juice (this is a Southern trick).

Use a heavy-bottomed pot with a tight lid. Bring the rice to a boil, then cover it tightly and turn down to a low simmer, 20 minutes for white rice and 45 minutes for brown (unless it has been soaked first—see quick-cooking brown rice below). Turn the heat off and leave the pot tightly covered until you are ready to serve it. (This is known as the "total absorption" method and preserves nutrients the best.) Long grain rice should be fluffed with a fork before serving.

Leftover rice, especially short grain, can be used in *Hash* (p. 133), or as a crust for savory pies and quiches.

Quick-Cooking Brown Rice: You can buy quick-cooking brown rice in boxes now, and it can be a real time-saver. However, it can be expensive if you use it all the time. You can shave 25 minutes off the cooking time of regular brown rice, though, if you plan ahead.

Simply soak the brown rice (any kind) in its measured cooking water for AT LEAST 4 hours before cooking. The best way to do this is to measure the rice and water, and any seasonings you might want to use, into the cooking pot in the morning. Turn on the heat under the pot before you start the rest of the meal. As soon as it comes to a boil, turn it down to a low simmer, cover, and cook for 20 minutes, while you make the rest of the meal.

Pressure Cooking Rice: I love my pressure cooker for beans, but I prefer the stove-top method of cooking rice to pressure cooking, because with the stove-top method the rice comes out dry and separate and requires no watching. In my experiments, both white and brown rice took quite a bit longer to cook than any of the books I consulted recommended. To tell you the truth, I thought it was more trouble than it was worth, (even for risotto, which I found took longer to cook than the books recommended, and then required about 10 minutes cooking without pressure, as well). But, if you'd like to try making brown rice in your pressure cooker (this would still take over 30 minutes for unsoaked brown rice), consult *Great Cooking Under Pressure* by Lorna Sass.

Microwaving Rice: There is not much time saved by using a microwave oven for cooking rice (but, in the case of risotto, it eliminates stirring and a dirty pot). If you want to use it for rice, consult a microwave cookbook.

Electric Rice Cookers: These can be programmed when you leave the house to turn on at a certain time later in the day. Follow the directions that come with your cooker. Electric rice cookers shut themselves off when the rice is done, but keep it warm. You can also steam foods above the rice.

kedegeree

Serves 4

1½ c. long grain white rice (basmati or converted are good), or quick-cooking brown rice

2 c. vegetarian broth plus ¼ c. water

1 medium onion, thinly sliced

2 c. (10 oz.) commercial smoked tofu, chopped, or *Smoky Tofu* (p. 30)

1-3 tsp. garam masala or curry powder

½ c. minced fresh parsley or cilantro

½ c. soymilk

pinch cayenne

salt and freshly ground pepper, to taste

per serving: calories: 269, protein: 13 gm., fat: 4 gm., carbohydrates: 45 gm.

Kedegeree is an Indian dish which is growing in popularity here in the West. It is usually eaten for breakfast, but it makes a great brunch, lunch, or supper dish. Instead of the smoked haddock customarily used in this recipe, we use smoked tofu.

In a medium saucepan, bring the rice, broth, and water to a boil, cover tightly, turn down the heat, and simmer for 15 minutes.

In the meantime, steam-fry the onion in a large, nonstick skillet until it begins to brown and soften. Add the smoked tofu and curry powder, and steam-fry for a few minutes. Add the parsley or cilantro, then the cooked rice, soymilk, and cayenne. Stir until the soymilk is absorbed and the whole dish is heated (this just takes a minute or two). Taste for salt and pepper.

quick smoky tofu

If you do not have commercial smoked tofu, or homemade *Smoky Tofu* on hand, you can make a very satisfactory, quick version by cutting up 10 oz. of reduced-fat, extra-firm tofu into small dice, placing in a nonstick skillet over high heat, and adding a mixture of ¼ c. water, 1 T. soy sauce, and 1 tsp. liquid smoke. Steam-fry until all the liquid is absorbed and the cubes begin to brown. This just takes a couple of minutes.

peruvian-style coriander rice with peas

Serves 6
(soy-free)

1 large onion, minced
OPTIONAL: **1 red bell pepper, seeded and diced**
2 T. minced pickled or canned jalapeño
6 large cloves garlic, minced
2 T. minced fresh cilantro, or 1 T. dried
1 T. ground coriander
1 tsp. ground cumin
2 c. long grain basmati or converted white rice
2 c. boiling water with 3 vegetarian bouillon cubes
1 c. dark beer, ale, stout, or non-alcoholic beer
1 c. frozen peas
freshly ground pepper, to taste
OPTIONAL ADDITIONS **(use one):**
> **1 (15 oz.) can chick-peas or corn, drained (1½ c. cooked)**
> **1 c. textured vegetable protein chunks, reconstituted (p. 26)**
> **1 lb. small, whole button mushrooms, browned**
> **2 c. seitan, *Breast of Tofu* (p. 29), or commercial, savory baked tofu or tempeh, or other poultry substitute, cut into cubes and browned in a nonstick pan**
> **1 or 2 cans Chinese vegetarian "roast duck" (mun chai'ya), rinsed and drained**

My father was Peruvian, so I have "veganized" several well-known Peruvian dishes. This one is adapted from arroz con pato, or rice with duck, a dish which resembles the ubiquitous Spanish or South American arroz con pollo (rice with chicken), but without the tomatoes. It makes a great side or light main dish as is, or you can add some vegetarian protein to make it a hearty main dish.

In a large, nonstick or lightly oiled heavy skillet with a tight-fitting lid, steam-fry the onion, bell pepper (if using), jalapeño, and garlic until it begins to brown a bit. Add the cilantro, coriander, and cumin, and steam-fry for a minute. Add the raw rice and steam-fry briefly. Pour in the hot water with bouillon, beer, peas, pepper, and any optional ingredients. Bring to a boil, cover, and cook for 15-20 minutes until the rice is done. Taste for salt and pepper.

per serving: calories: 184, protein: 4 gm., fat: 0 gm., carbohydrates: 40 gm.

Arroz sin Pollo: Omit the jalapeño and beer, and add 1 (28 oz.) can of diced tomatoes with juice and ¼ tsp. of Spanish saffron (or 1 tsp. American saffron). Use any Optional Addition except the corn.

For a Spanish-style dish, use short or medium-grain rice, such as Italian arborio.

For the South American version, use long grain rice, basmati, or converted rice, and add 2 green peppers, seeded and diced.

Jambalaya: Make as for "Arroz sin Pollo," using long grain rice, but omit the saffron and peas. Use any Optional Addition, except the corn. Instead of chick-peas, you could use black-eyed peas or small red beans. Use 2 large onions and add 2 green peppers, seeded and diced. Add 2 bay leaves, 2 tsp. dried thyme, 2 tsp. dried basil, and 2 tsp. Louisiana hot sauce.

Quick and Easy "Paella": This is not authentic, but it's good! Use medium grain rice, such as arborio. Omit the jalapeños, cilantro, coriander, and cumin. Omit the beer and use dry white wine or 3 c. hot water in total. Add ¼ tsp. Spanish saffron (or 1 tsp. American saffron), ¼ c. minced fresh parsley, and 3 chopped tomatoes or 1 (28 oz.) can diced tomatoes, well-drained. Use either one or two of the Optional Additions, except the corn, or add ¾ c. cooked chick-peas, 1 c. frozen, small, whole green beans, 2 c. sliced frozen carrots, and 8 canned or frozen artichoke hearts, in addition to the peas called for. (Thaw frozen vegetables first under hot running water in a colander.) Serve with lemon wedges.

COOKING NOTE: Although many books call for long grain rice in a Spanish paella or arroz con pollo recipe, the Spanish use a rice grown in Valencia, similar to Italian arborio rice, which is a good substitute. Long grain rice produces an entirely different texture, much appreciated in South America.

quick stove-top risotto

Serves 3-4
(soy-free)

1 large onion, minced
3 cloves garlic, minced
1 c. arborio rice
2½ c. hot vegetarian broth (you can also use fresh vegetable juice, such as carrot or celery, for some of the liquid)
½ c. dry white wine, dry vermouth, dry sherry, or non-alcoholic alternative (or more broth or juice—3 c. liquid in total)
½-1 tsp. dried herb of choice, or 1 T. or more fresh basil, sage, rosemary, oregano, etc.
¼ c. non-dairy "milk"
OPTIONAL: ¼ c. soy Parmesan
salt and pepper, to taste

per serving: calories: 222, protein: 4 gm., fat: 1 gm., carbohydrates: 40 gm.

1½-3 c. chopped fresh or frozen vegetables, such as:
asparagus
broccoli
carrots
celery
cooked or canned beans
green beans
green onions
greens (including arugula)
grilled eggplant
leeks
leftover roasted vegetables
mushrooms
peas
roasted red peppers
soaked dried tomatoes (p. 46)
summer or winter squash
zucchini

OPTIONAL ADDITIONS:
½ tsp. dried red chile pepper flakes
¼ c. chopped vegetarian "ham" or "back bacon"
½ c. chopped, smoked tofu or *Smoky Tofu* (p. 30)
1 T. grated lemon zest
¼ c. minced parsley

This is a departure from the usual stove-top risotto where you stir the liquid in a little at a time (taking about 30 minutes and a lot of attention). Subsequently this method isn't quite as creamy, but it's still deliciously rich-tasting and saves a lot of time and effort. To have the creamiest result, make sure you use Italian arborio rice.

Risotto can be made with almost any vegetable you have around. I rarely make it the same way twice. It makes an excellent main dish as well as "side." No butter or oil is necessary, and a little bit of soy Parmesan is optional.

Steam-fry the garlic, onion, and any optional vegetables that you want to cook with the risotto in a nonstick, medium saucepan until the onion begins to soften. Alternatively, you can cook any vegetables separately so they will have more texture—steam, grill, roast, broil, or steam-fry—just to the point of tenderness. You can do this while the risotto is cooking, and then add them to the risotto after it is cooked.

Stir in the rice and then the remaining ingredients, except the soy Parmesan, non-dairy "milk," and any cooked optional vegetables and additions you are using. Make sure the broth is hot when you add it to the rice. Bring everything to a boil, then turn down to medium, and simmer uncovered for 15 minutes, stirring now and then. Remove from the heat, add the non-dairy "milk," any cooked optional vegetables, and any optional additions you are using. Stir until the "milk" is absorbed, and serve. Add soy Parmesan, if you wish.

Form leftover risotto into patties, or smooth it into a flat pan, chill, and cut into rounds, squares, or triangles. Brown in a nonstick skillet, or bake or grill like *Polenta* (p. 169).

NOTE: Risotto should not be like a porridge. The rice grains should be separate, and slightly chewy in the middle (but not hard) and creamy on the outside. RISOTTO SHOULD BE EATEN RIGHT AWAY. It doesn't sit or reheat well (except as patties).

microwave risotto

This is one situation where you CAN save time to cook rice in a microwave oven. With this method, you can have creamy, savory risotto in under half an hour with no stirring. It's actually no faster than the stove-top method described on p. 166-167, but it requires a little less attention. Another advantage is that you can cook it right in the serving dish, so you have no dirty pot!

Read through the whole recipe for *Quick Stove-Top Risotto*. Use the same ingredients, but use only 2½ c. liquid in total (all broth, broth mixed with vegetable juice, or 2 c. broth, broth/juice and ½ c. wine). This liquid doesn't have to be hot.

Place the onions and garlic in a medium-sized, microwave-safe casserole. Cover and cook on high for 3 minutes. Add the rice, liquid, any optional vegetables that you are adding at this point, and herbs. Stir well, cover, and cook on high for 14-15 minutes. (This was how long it took in a 900 watt oven. If your oven is a lower wattage, cook a few minutes longer.) Carefully uncover and stir in the non-dairy "milk," any cooked optional vegetables you are adding at this point, and any optional additions you might be using. Cover and let stand 3 minutes. Taste for salt and pepper. Add soy Parmesan, if you like.

polenta and other cornmeal concoctions

Polenta is the Italian name for savory cornmeal mush. It sounds mundane, but it's a perfect contrast for spicy sauces or mushroom stews. It's the same as the traditional cornmeal mush topping for tamale pie, by the way, and is called "coush-coush" in Louisiana. It can be creamy and soft when served fresh, or dense and firm when allowed to cool, then sliced and baked, grilled, or browned in a skillet. It's a great change from potatoes, pasta, bread, or rice.

There's really no need to stand and stir polenta for an hour, as was done in the past by Italian housewives. Use ordinary, inexpensive yellow cornmeal and a double boiler, pressure cooker, or microwave to make polenta effortlessly, and even quickly.

Serve fresh polenta either with soy Parmesan and herbs for a side dish, or as a main dish topped with spaghetti sauce, vegetarian Italian "sausage," or stew. Top casseroles with it instead of potatoes. Smooth it with the back of a spoon into an oiled pie pan, and let it cool, to bake as a "crust" for quiches and other savory pie mixtures.

Make an impressive, molded polenta by making the mush as for firm polenta (p. 169), then scooping it into a well-oiled mold, such as you might use for a jellied salad. Let it stand 5-10 minutes to firm up, then invert it onto a serving dish, and serve right away, or reheat later, uncovered, in a microwave for 10 minutes. Slice it either with a sharp knife or with a taut string, as the Italians do.

Firm, sliced polenta can baked, grilled, or browned in a pan to be served for dinner with any topping you might use for potatoes, pasta, or rice. You can even use thin slices as a substitute for lasagne noodles. For an appetizer, grill polenta slices, and top with *Pesto* (p. 77) and other crostini or bruschetta toppings (p. 53).

instant polenta

If you're really in a hurry, there is instant polenta available. Just bring it to a boil with water, and it's ready. There's also ready-to-eat polenta in plastic, airtight tube bags (in various flavors). Just slice it and bake, brown, or microwave. You can also press it into a pie pan, and fill it with your favorite spicy mixture, then heat. Expect to pay premium price for it, though. And the flavor and texture are lacking.

basic double-boiler or pressure cooker polenta

For a soft, creamy polenta, use the larger amount of liquid. For a firm or molded polenta, use the lesser amount. Soft, creamy polenta will still firm up when it's cold. For a savory polenta, add low-salt vegetarian broth powder and herbs, etc. Use yellow cornmeal.

Servings	4	6	8
Cornmeal	1 c.	1½	2 c.
COLD Water	2-4 c.	3-4½ c.	4-6 c.
Salt	¼ tsp.	½ tsp.	¾ tsp.
Broth Powder	1 T.	1½ T.	2 T.

Mix the cornmeal with the COLD water, salt, and optional broth powder. Pouring hot water into dry cornmeal will create lumps. For a richer, creamier polenta, use all or part non-dairy "milk" instead of water. For a "polenta" to use with Mexican foods, use masa harina (Mexican corn tortilla flour) instead of cornmeal.

Double-Boiler Method: Mix the cornmeal and water in the top of a double boiler. Set the BOTTOM of the double boiler to boil with water in it. Place the TOP of the double boiler directly over high heat, and bring to a boil quickly, stirring almost constantly with a whisk or wooden spoon to prevent sticking and clumping. IMMEDIATELY after it boils, place it in the bottom part of the double boiler over the simmering water. Let simmer 15-20 minutes, partially covered, and stirring now and then until the mush is creamy and smooth (for soft) or very thick and not gritty anymore (for firm).

Serve immediately or pour into a well-oiled mold, loaf pan, or flat baking pan. Let set 5-10 minutes for a hot mold, or chill (even for several days) if you want to slice it. You can quick-chill it by spreading it no more than ½" thick in a flat pan or in muffin tins, and placing it in the freezer for a few minutes.

Pressure-Cooker Method: Mix the polenta, cold water, salt, and optional broth powder in a heat-proof or stainless steel bowl or casserole that will fit into your pressure cooker. Cover with foil. Fold a long piece of heavy foil into a 2"-wide strip, run it under the casserole/bowl, and use that to lift the container in and out of the cooker. Place the casserole/bowl on a rack over 1"-2" of water in the bottom of your cooker. Bring to 15 lbs. pressure over high heat, then turn down just enough to maintain this pressure, and cook 10 minutes. Remove from the heat and let rest 5 minutes, then quick-release the pressure under cold running water. Stir the polenta and proceed as above to serve or mold.

Microwave Method: Use the amounts for 6 servings. Whisk the ingredients together in a large, microwave-safe bowl or casserole. Cover and cook on high for 5 minutes. Whisk the polenta. Cover again and cook on high for 3 minutes. Whisk again. Cover once more and cook again for 3 minutes. Let stand 1 minute, then proceed as above to serve or mold.

To Brown Firm Polenta Slices: Either grill or broil them 3"-4" from the heat source until speckled with browned spots. You can also brown them over high to medium-high heat in a nonstick skillet, or place them on a lightly oiled or nonstick cookie sheet, and bake them at 450°F for 10-15 minutes.

Savory Polenta: Stir dried or fresh herbs, chopped dried tomatoes or roasted red peppers, a bit of soy bacon bits or chopped veggie "ham" or "back bacon," parsley, chopped garlic, pepper or chile flakes, and/or soy Parmesan into the polenta as it cooks. Use the broth powder.

Gnocchi (pronounced nyoh-kee): For this Italian dumpling dish, use the broth powder and make the firm polenta. To the 6-serving amount of Basic Polenta, add: 2-3 crushed cloves garlic, a few dashes of black pepper, and ⅓ c. minced fresh parsley. Pour the polenta about ½" thick onto an oiled cookie sheet with sides (a jelly roll pan). Chill until firm; use a freezer for speed.

To serve, cut into 2" squares, then cut the squares in half to make triangles. Overlap the triangles in an oiled, shallow baking pan. Sprinkle with soy Parmesan and/or drizzle with *Melty Pizza Cheeze* (p. 42). Bake at 400°F for 10-15 minutes. Serve with a marinara (Italian tomato) sauce or your favorite, low-fat, vegetarian spaghetti sauce.

Scrapple: Scrapple is an old Pennsylvania Dutch dish that is usually made with pork scraps, but it's easy to make a delicious vegetarian version. It's basically a firm polenta with the addition of herbs and vegetarian sausage. It's good for breakfast, lunch, or supper. Use the broth powder in making the firm polenta. To the 6-serving amount of Basic Polenta, add: ⅛ tsp. EACH dried sage, thyme, or savory, and black pepper, and 2 c. crumbled, cooked, low-fat vegetarian commercial or homemade breakfast "sausage" (p. 28). Instead of the "sausage," you could also use ground or chopped, commercial savory baked or smoked tofu, *Smoky Tofu* (p. 30), ground seitan, or commercial "ready-ground" savory tofu. You can also add grated or chopped apple, steam-fried grated or chopped onion, and/or celery, if you wish. Pour the cooked mixture into an oiled loaf pan, and chill. Slice it about ½" thick and broil, grill, or brown on a nonstick pan. Serve with maple syrup, gravy, ketchup, or applesauce.

potato dishes

Potatoes are well-loved around our house, despite the plethora of exotic alternatives available to us. They are cheap, nutritious, always available, comforting, versatile, and just plain good to eat! Our three large sons reach for the potato box any time of the day. I gave you a couple of methods for quick-baking potatoes on pps. 153, plus some ideas for toppings. This chapter offers potato dishes that are more like "sides," but they can all be used as main dishes if you're a potato afficionado or looking for a low-cost, quick-to-cook meal.

Remember to use mealy, mature Russet baking potatoes, Netted Gem (a Canadian variety), Idaho Bakers, Yukon Gold, California Russets, All Blue, Peruvian Blue, or Peruvian Purple. These varieties are best for baking, mashing, barbecuing, puréeing for creamed soups, and using in breads. They are also good for oven-fries, as are Kennebecs, Norchips, Mononas, and the yellow Desiree.

The "waxy," thin-skinned types (White Rose, Yellow Finnish, Yellow Rose, Blue Shetland, Delta Blue, new red varieties, and new white varieties), are good for boiling, steaming, and in stews, salads, scalloped potatoes, and soups, as they hold their shape. "Long white" varieties, like Explorers, are also excellent for grating and shredding.

Some potatoes can be used as an all-purpose potato. Good examples of these are Maine potatoes like Katahdins, Superiors, Sebagos, Irish Cobblers, and Chippewas (also known as round whites or Aroostooks), and new varieties like BelRus, Norgold Russet, Yellow Bintje, Nooksaks, and new Russets, which are shipped in early summer instead of fall, like mature Russets.

Yellow varieties have a rich, "buttery" taste. The "blue" varieties actually range in color from dark blue to deep purple.

basic boiled and mashed potatoes

Boiled potatoes are most nutritious when left unpeeled. Use organic potatoes, if you can, because the nutritious skin can also harbor unwanted pesticides if the potatoes have been sprayed. If you don't want skins in your mashed potatoes, and you are too rushed to slip off the skins from the hot, cooked potatoes, you can peel them first.

Scrub the potatoes under running water with a firm brush, and cut off any bad spots or green skin. Cut them into pieces more or less the same size, or leave them whole if they are quite small. Cover them with cold water (or broth, for more flavor), and add a little salt, if you wish, bring to a boil, and simmer gently for 15-20 minutes. Some people cover the pot and some people don't. If you cook more than 2 lbs. of potatoes in one pot, they will take longer to cook. New potatoes should be added to the boiling water.

As soon as they are tender, drain them and return them to the pot. To remove excess moisture, cover them with a clean tea towel, and top with a lid for a few minutes.

Mash them well with a potato masher, then add about ½ c. soymilk or other nondairy "milk" per 6 medium potatoes. Whip with a wooden spoon, and season with salt and white pepper.

For extra flavor, boil a whole head of peeled garlic with the potatoes, and mash it in.

Serve "as is," or stir in:
  minced fresh parsley or other herbs, such as mint or dill
  steam-fried minced onion (just soft, or cooked to the brown, caramelized stage, p. 44)
  chopped chives or green onions
  soy bacon bits or chips
  a little dry white wine or sherry
  cayenne
  dry mustard
  nutritional yeast flakes
  lemon juice (and/or lemon zest)
  chipotle chiles
  Tofu Cream Cheeze (p. 36)
  Soy-Free Cream Cheeze (p. 38)
  Tofu-Cashew Sour Cream (p. 36)
  Tofu Sour Cream (p. 35), or *Soy-Free Sour Cream* (p. 33)
  soy Parmesan
  curry powder or other spices
  Pesto (p. 77)

You can add cooked, puréed, roasted, grilled, or leftover vegetables to mashed potatoes. Try mixing them half and half with mashed cooked carrots, winter squash, sweet potatoes, parsnips, turnips, rutabagas, or celeriac.

Mixing cooked mashed potatoes and greens is popular in many countries and very nutritious and delicious too. This can be as simple as a package of frozen chopped spinach, cooked, thawed, and squeezed, and then added to the potatoes.

pressure-steamed and microwaved potatoes

Steaming produces a potato with lovely texture and flavor, but conventional steaming takes longer than boiling (which just squeaks into the quick category). You can steam potatoes quickly in either your microwave oven or pressure cooker to use for oven- or pan-frying, eating like plain, boiled potatoes, or mashing.

To micro-steam, place the potatoes (new, small ones, or cut into 2"-3" chunks) in a microwave-safe casserole or glass pie dish. Add about ¼ c. of water, cover, and cook on high for 8-10 minutes. For mashed potatoes, cut them into large dice, and use 1 c. water. Cook 10 minutes or more until very tender and drain. This is a good cooking method for blue or purple varieties, which tend to fall apart easily.

To pressure-steam, place them in a steamer basket (on a rack, if necessary) over a couple of inches of hot water in your pressure cooker, and lock the lid in place. Bring it quickly to 15 lbs. pressure over high heat, then turn the heat down just low enough to keep the pressure at 15 lbs.

5 or 6 oz., quartered	= 7 min.
4 oz., whole	= 10 min.
4 oz., halved	= 7 min.
1" cubes	= 3 min.
1" slices	= 4 min.
2 oz., whole new	= 8 min.
1 oz., new	= 5 min.

IMMEDIATELY quick-release the steam under cold running water, and remove the lid so that they don't overcook.

For pre-cooking ¼" slices or large dices of potatoes, simply bring the pot up to pressure, and then quick-release under cold running water.

spicy chinese potatoes

For each person, cut a medium peeled potato into ½" dice. Add it to a hot, nonstick skillet with ½ chopped onion, 1 minced clove garlic, and 2 diced green onions. Steam-fry for a few minutes until the mixture starts to brown. Add ½ c. water or vegetarian broth, and 1 tsp. EACH soy sauce (or alternate, p. 13) and Szechuan hot bean paste (Chinese chile bean paste), or soy-free chile paste. Add ½ tsp. vinegar, if desired.

Cover and simmer 5 minutes, or until the potatoes are tender. Add salt and pepper, to taste.

spicy spanish potatoes

Steam-fry the potatoes in a nonstick skillet until slightly browned, seasoning them to taste with garlic granules, paprika, dried red chile pepper flakes or chile powder, salt, and ground cumin.

masala potatoes

Serves 4
(soy-free)

**3 large (8 oz.) cooked potatoes, peeled
    and cubed**
1 or 2 large onions, minced
**1 T. minced fresh gingerroot, or 1 tsp.
    powdered ginger**
**OPTIONAL: ½ green pepper, seeded and
    diced**
1 tsp. black or yellow mustard seed
1 tsp. garam masala or curry powder
½ tsp. salt
1½ tsp. lemon juice

per serving: calories: 167, protein: 2 gm.,
fat: 0 gm., carbohydrates: 39 gm.

*Use as a spicy side dish, or roll up in whole
wheat chapatis or tortillas, and top with* Tofu
Yogurt *or* Tofu Sour Cream *(p. 35),* Tofu-
Cashew Sour Cream *(p. 36), or* Soy-Free Sour
Cream *(p. 33) for a quick meal.*

In a large, nonstick skillet, steam-fry the
onions, fresh ginger, and optional green pepper
with the mustard seed until the onion is tender.
Add the potatoes, masala or curry, salt, and
lemon juice, and steam-fry until the potatoes
are hot.

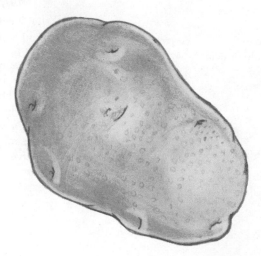

quick oven-fries, roasted potatoes, or potato wedges

Start with leftover baked, boiled, or steamed potatoes. You can also cook the amount you want quickly by micro- or pressure-steaming as directed on p. 153. Cut the potatoes to the size you want before cooking to save time—French fry shapes, large wedges, cubes, or whatever. Place them on a nonstick or lightly oiled cookie sheet (or sheets), in 1 layer. Brush them with some commercial or home-made, non-fat vinaigrette, Italian-style dressing, barbecue sauce or glaze (any kind—even an Oriental type such as *Teriyaki*, p. 108), or a lemon vinaigrette with oregano for "Greek roasted potatoes." Broil them about 3"-4" from the heat for several minutes, until they are nicely browned (watch them carefully). Turn them over and repeat the brushing and broiling. Serve immediately.

Variations: Sprinkle the potatoes, after brushing with the dressing or sauce with:

garlic granules
fresh chopped or dried herbs such as sage,
    rosemary, tarragon, basil, or oregano
Cajun seasoning
Louisiana hot sauce
soy Parmesan
grated lemon or orange zest
pepper, cayenne, or chile powder

quick oven french fries (chips)

If you have a French fry cutter (many food processors have one with the basic cutting and shredding attachments), you can make crispy oven French fries with NO OIL in 25 minutes (this includes preparation)!

Preheat the oven to 500°F. Select long, large (8 oz. or so) potatoes, if you can. These can just be shaved a bit on their fat middles, so that they fit right into the feeder tube of your processor. Four large potatoes will just fill two 10" x 15" cookie sheets. Scrub the potatoes. I leave the skins on and just trim when necessary. Spread the fries in one layer on lightly oiled or nonstick cookie sheets.

Bake 10 minutes, then flip them over, and bake 10 minutes more. If you have extra cookie sheets, the quickest way to flip them over is just to place another nonstick or oiled cookie sheet over the one with the fries, flip the whole thing over, and remove the first sheet. Sprinkle with salt and pepper or other seasonings, such as Cajun.

That's it! Golden, crispy, no-fat fries!

"buffalo potato wedges"

"Hot Wings" fans, take note! Brush large potato wedges with vinaigrette, and sprinkle with salt and cayenne pepper, or Cajun seasoning, to taste. Broil as directed above. Dip the crusty wedges into *Vegetable Dip* (p. 48)—you can add a bit of crumbled, white Chinese fermented tofu (doufu-ru) to make it more like the traditional blue cheese dressing or dip. Or you can use a spicy, ketchup-style chile sauce; mix ketchup and salsa together, half and half. Serve with celery sticks.

potato pancakes

Serves 6 (makes about 30 pancakes)
(soy-free)

**9 medium Russet potatoes, peeled and
    grated, or 7 c. fat-free frozen,
    grated potatoes**
1 large onion, peeled and grated
¾ c. whole wheat flour
⅓ c. nutritional yeast flakes
1 T. baking powder
1½ tsp. salt
¼ tsp. white pepper

per serving: calories: 279, protein: 7 gm.,
fat: 0 gm., carbohydrates: 61 gm.

Mix the onion and potato together well in a large bowl. Add the other ingredients and mix well.

You can cook these on several large, heavy nonstick or lightly oiled skillets over medium-high heat. Another option is to use a nonstick, electric pancake griddle—this accommodates quite a few pancakes, and they cook evenly.

Place ¼ c. of the potato mixture for each pancake onto the preheated griddle or skillets, and flatten into thin pancakes with a spatula. Cover them with lids or foil (I use inverted cookie sheets over the griddle) until the bottoms are golden-brown. Then flip them over and cook, uncovered, until the second side is golden-brown. Serve hot with applesauce and *Tofu Sour Cream* (p. 35), *Tofu-Cashew Sour Cream* (p. 36), or *Soy-Free Sour Cream* (p. 33).

Oven-Baked Potato Pancakes: Preheat the oven to 500°F. Flatten the pancakes on lightly oiled or nonstick cookie sheets. Bake 15 minutes, then turn over, and bake 5-6 minutes more.

Variations: You can use a mixture of ½ potato and ½ carrot, yam, turnip, parsnip, zucchini, or winter squash, or some grated, peeled broccoli stems or radishes, along with the onion. Add some dried dillweed, if you like. You can also add some crushed garlic and/or dried herbs, caraway seeds, or chives, or Indian herbs and spices, such as cumin and turmeric. You can also add 1 c. of cooked, minced greens, or some squeezed, dry soy bacon bits or minced veggie "ham" or "back bacon."

low-fat homefries

Start with diced, cooked potatoes (either leftover or quickly micro- or pressure-steam according to the directions on pps. 153)—they can be boiled, steamed, or baked. For each 2 medium potatoes, steam-fry a chopped or sliced medium onion, in a nonstick pan until it starts to soften. Add the potatoes and steam-fry, using vegetarian broth as the liquid, until the potatoes begin to brown. Season with salt and pepper. Serve plain or with gravy, ketchup, or salsa. For a main dish, drizzle with *Melty Pizza Cheeze* (p. 42) or sprinkle with soy Parmesan, and place under the broiler until bubbly. (This is especially good when you add garlic and chile to the potatoes.)

Add the following optional ingredients to the cooking potatoes:
    chopped garlic or garlic granules
    chopped jalapeños or chile pepper flakes
        or chile powder
    Cajun seasoning
    diced green or red bell pepper
    ground cumin
    chopped cilantro or parsley or other green herbs
    a few squirts of fresh lemon or lime juice
        and/or a sprinkle of soy sauce

oven-crisped hash browns

Preheat the oven to 500°F. Mound grated potatoes or fat-free, frozen grated potatoes (you can add some grated onion if you like) on nonstick cookie sheets, about 6 mounds per sheet. Flatten the mounds with a spatula, sprinkle with salt and pepper (and other seasonings, such as Cajun, if you like), and bake on the lower shelf of the oven for 10 minutes, or until browned on the bottom. Turn over and bake 10 minutes more.

If you're really pressed for time, use fat-free, frozen grated potatoes.

easy waffle iron hash browns

Grate potatoes medium-fine and squeeze out the excess juice in a cloth. You can add some grated onion if you like. Pack the grated potatoes into a hot, nonstick waffle iron, brushed or sprayed lightly with oil. (Use about 1 c. for each 4" square.) Sprinkle with salt and pepper, or other seasonings, such as Cajun. Close the lid and cook about 10-20 minutes, or until as golden brown and crispy as you like.

If you're really pressed for time, use fat-free, frozen grated potatoes.

cooking sweet potatoes

Contrary to how they may be labeled, orange-fleshed sweet potatoes are not "yams"—yams are less sweet and more earthy. Sweet potatoes are very nutritious and scrumptious. Babies love them. They are delicious barbecued or grilled.

To microwave whole sweet potatoes, prick them with a fork and place them like the spokes of a wheel on paper towelling on a microwave carousel. Two (5-7 oz.) sweet potatoes take 5-9 minutes; 4 take 8-13 minutes. Cut large potatoes in half.

To "micro-steam" sweet potato chunks, cut 1 lb. into 1½" pieces, place in a microwave-safe dish or pie plate, add 2 T. water, cover, and cook on high for 5 minutes.

When pressure-steaming sweet potatoes, large quartered ones take 5-7 minutes at high pressure (15 lbs.); ¼" slices take 2-3 minutes. Bring pressure down quickly under cold running water.

Conventional steaming is a quick way to cook sweet potatoes too. Peeled ¼"-1" cubes or strips can be steamed in a steamer basket over boiling water for 12-15 minutes.

peruvian sweet potato chips
(camote frito)

Serves 6
(soy-free)

**4-6 medium orange-fleshed sweet
potatoes, peeled**

per serving: calories: 158, protein: 2 gm.,
fat: 0 gm., carbohydrates: 38 gm.

*Sweet potato fries are sold by street vendors in
the towns and cities of Peru, where my father
came from.*

Preheat the oven to 500°F. Cut the sweet potatoes into ⅛" thick wedges, like French fries.
(Use a French fry cutter, if you have one.) Place
the "fries" on two nonstick or lightly oiled
cookie sheets. Bake for 5-7 minutes, then turn
over and bake 5-7 minutes longer, or until light
golden and crispy outside and soft in the middle. Sprinkle with coarse salt and serve hot.

glossary

Agar: Also known as agar-agar or kanten (the Japanese word), this vegetarian gelling agent is made from a seaweed. Like gelatin, it is tasteless and has no calories, so it can be used instead of gelatin in fruit gels and savory aspic. Unlike gelatin, it can set at room temperature. It is widely available in natural food stores in the form of powder, flakes, or bars.

To gel 2 cups of liquid, use 1 teaspoon of agar powder, 2 tablespoons of agar flakes, or about half a bar of kanten. As a comparison, a tablespoon or packet of unflavored, regular gelatin will gel 2 cups of liquid. To use agar flakes instead of agar powder in a recipe, use six times as much.

Certain things interfere with the gelling of agar—vinegar and oxalic acid (found in chocolate and spinach), for instance. Fruit acids may soften the gel somewhat—you'll have to experiment with fruit juices to see if you need more than the recommended amount to achieve the degree of firmness that you like. Try using half again as much agar, especially with citrus, tomato, and pineapple.

Bulgur Wheat: This quick-cooking wheat product is of ancient origin. Wheat kernels are boiled, dried, and cracked. The resulting bulgur needs only to be cooked for 10 to 15 minutes (1 part bulgur to 2 parts liquid).

Chinese Dried Mushrooms or Shiitake: Oriental black mushrooms add wonderful flavor to marinades, stews, stir-fries, gravies, sauces, and soups. Store the mushrooms in a cool, dry place. To rehydrate them, soak them in boiling water to cover for about 30 minutes, then drain and discard the stems. Use the soaking water in cooking.

Chipolte Chiles in Adobado Sauce: These are smoked jalapeño chiles canned in tomato sauce, available in Latin American markets and some supermarkets and natural food stores. They not only add heat to a dish, but a delicious, smoky flavor. Try them in chiles, dips, and salsas.

Cornstarch: Many natural foods cookbooks call for the use of arrowroot powder instead of cornstarch, implying that it is somehow nutritionally superior to cornstarch—it's not. Both are highly refined and not particularly nutritious—arrowroot is much more expensive than cornstarch, however. Since we use only small amounts as a thickener, and because cornstarch is more stable, I call for cornstarch.

Cornstarch and arrowroot are not completely interchangeable. Cornstarch needs about 30 seconds of boiling to remove the starchy taste; arrowroot turns clear in very hot liquid without boiling and has no starchy aftertaste.

When arrowroot cools, it becomes rather slimy, so be sure to use cornstarch in recipes that will be served chilled. Arrowroot, on the other hand, is useful for making very glossy, dark hot sauces without fat.

Mix either arrowroot or cornstarch with COLD liquid until smooth before heating or adding to hot food.

Dried Mushrooms: Dried mushrooms and, especially, the soaking broth from reconstituting them (p. 46) can add rich, intense flavor to certain dishes. For Oriental dishes, use dried shiitakes or the less expensive, but similar, Chinese black mushrooms.

For Italian, French, and other European dishes, use dried porcini or cèpes mushrooms. The European varieties are extremely costly, however, so you might prefer to use the more reasonably priced South American boletus, which are still quite good. Make sure that they are brown, rather than black, in color, and still flexible. (You don't want totally dessicated chips.) The soaking broth from porcinis can be substituted for rich beef stock, and you can cook it down by half for an intense flavoring extract.

If you can't find porcinis in your area (see the Mail Order Sources on p. 186), you can use Oriental dried mushrooms, but be aware that the flavor isn't as sweet or intense as porcinis, even the inexpensive ones. You can get a more intense flavor by cooking the soaking broth down until it is reduced by half.

Dulse Flakes: Nutritious little flakes of this reddish-purple sea vegetable, dulse lends a mild "seafood" flavor to chowders, etc. The flakes are much less expensive than the whole dried pieces, and you need only about one-fourth the amount. Available in health food stores.

Garlic Granules: You may wonder why I call for garlic granules instead of garlic powder when I don't use fresh garlic. This is because garlic granules are made of ground, dried garlic, and garlic power often has starch added, so it is not of the same quality. Garlic granules are available in most supermarkets and in the bulk spice department of natural foods stores.

Hoisin Sauce, Chinese Black Bean Sauce, Chinese Brown Bean Sauce, and Szechuan Hot Bean Paste: These popular Chinese condiments are readily available in Chinese grocery stores or the Asian section of large supermarkets. Light miso can be a substitute for brown bean sauce. There is a chick-pea miso, made by Miso Master in Rutherford, N.C., that is available in some health food stores. Half dark miso and half liquid sweetener can substitute for hoisin sauce. Other chile pastes or sauces (some are pure chile, without any soy) can substitute for Szechuan hot bean paste (sometimes called Chinese chile bean paste). However, these substitutes will be lacking in that special Chinese flavor. There isn't really any substitute for Chinese black bean sauce (made from special, fermented black soybeans), except perhaps very dark soy sauce or mushroom soy sauce. To make a soy-free black bean sauce, you can use plain Chinese salted black beans, mashed with a fork and mixed with steam-fried garlic and some *Soy-Free Soy Sauce Replacement* (p. 13).

Instant Gluten Powder: Instant gluten powder (also known as vital wheat gluten, "Do-Pep," or pure gluten flour) is available in most natural food stores. The powder is made from gluten, the protein in wheat. Small amounts can be added to bread flour to improve it for bread-baking, or it can be mixed with cold liquid to make meat substitutes. The raw gluten is cooked in a flavored broth and is then known by the Japanese name "seitan."

Do not confuse instant gluten powder with something called "gluten flour." This product is refined wheat flour with gluten powder added. Make sure that it is vital wheat gluten that you are buying.

Kelp Powder: This pale green, slightly salty, mineral-rich, powdered sea vegetable lends a slightly "fishy" taste to chowders and to Southeast Asian foods that ordinarily call for fish sauce. Mix a pinch of kelp powder in with light soy sauce used measure-for-measure instead of the fish sauce. Available in natural food stores.

Liquid Smoke: This is a useful flavoring to replace the smoky taste of ham, bacon, etc., especially in bean dishes. New studies show that it does not contain carcinogenic impurities, as once thought.

Look for brands that are simply water and natural hickory smoke. Others also contain vinegar, brown sugar, and caramel coloring, but you have to use more to obtain the right results. Add just a few shakes to your dish, and taste to see if it is strong enough—you don't need much. It's available in most supermarkets, usually near the barbecue sauces.

Miso: Miso is a Japanese fermented soybean and grain paste (usually made with rice or barley) which is used as a soup base and a flavoring. It is salty but highly nutritious and valued for its digestive qualities. Unpasteurized miso contains beneficial bacteria similar to that in yogurt, so avoid heating it to the boiling point. If your natural foods store has a selection of misos, try them out to see which you like—there can be a number of varieties: dark, light, sweet, mellow, etc. When I call for miso, I'm referring to light brown rice or barley miso. When I call for "light miso," you can use a sweet white, mellow white, or mellow beige miso. Chick-pea miso is a soy-free substitute that can be used for either type. There is a chick-pea miso made by the Miso Master company in Rutherford, N. C., that is available in some health food stores.

Nutritional Yeast: Nutritional yeast is NOT the same thing as brewer's yeast or baking yeast. Nutritional yeast flakes have a cheesy taste and, when mixed with soy sauce or spices, also a rather "chickeny" flavor, so they are best used in savory dishes. I also use them in some baking to replace the rich taste of egg yolk.

Nutritional yeast is a concentrated source of protein, minerals, and B-vitamins, and contains no fat and few calories, so it is an important seasoning in vegan cooking. (Some brands have vitamin B_{12} added.) You might like to keep some on your table, like salt, for sprinkling on foods (delicious on popcorn!). You'll find it in natural foods stores, or you can obtain it from some mail order sources (p. 186).

Rice: Whenever possible, use brown rice. It takes longer to cook than white rice (unless you use expensive, "instant" brown rice), but it is superior in terms of fiber and nutrients. Brown rice takes about 45 minutes to cook. If you put the rice on before you start the rest of the meal, it'll be done by the time most things are cooked.

For quick-cooking brown rice, soak the brown rice in its cooking water for at least 4 hours (before you go to work, for instance). After soaking, it will cook in 20 minutes!

Long grain brown rice cooks up in fluffy, separate grains; short grain is stickier. There are some delicious varieties of brown rice besides these—brown basmati, Calmati or Texmati (which are very long-grained and aromatic), and wehani, a rust-colored, long grain brown rice with a popcorn aroma and the appearance of wild rice. Wehani is good mixed with regular, long grain brown rice.

If you prefer white rice, there are several good choices. White basmati is not only delicious, but is not polished. Converted (parboiled) rice is steamed before hulling, so that some of the nutrients from the bran are forced into the kernel. Under no circumstances use instant white rice.

Seitan: Seitan (pronounced say-tan) is the Japanese word for cooked, seasoned wheat gluten that is used as a meat substitute because of its chewy texture. It is available in the refrigerator section of most natural food stores or as a packaged mix to make your own. You can also find many canned versions in Oriental grocery stores (such as mun chai'ya, or vegetarian "roast duck"). Chinese Buddhists have been making incredible meat substitutes with wheat gluten for centuries.

Seitan is a great food particularly for vegetarians who are allergic to soy. If you can't buy the already prepared seitan, or you are allergic to the soy sauce that flavors it, Arrowhead Mills makes a Quick Seitan Mix. The Mail Order Catalog (see Mail Order Sources, p. 186) carries instant gluten flour and a book on cooking with and making seitan, plus seitan "chicken" and "sausage" mixes. My previous two books have seitan roast recipes.

Knox Mountain Farms (p. 186) has three fat-free, soy-free seitan mixes that are not instant, but would be handy for many people. There is a "Wheatball," "Sausage" (both made with gluten and bulgur wheat), and a "Chick 'n' Wheat" (made with gluten and chick-pea flour). You can use my *Soy-Free Soy Sauce or Tamari Replacement* on p. 13 instead of the soy sauce called for on the box as a seasoning.

Soy Bacon Bits or Chips: This condiment is widely available in grocery stores. It's made with soy flour, soy protein, and artificial and natural flavorings. It does have a bit of oil in it, but, since it is used in small amounts, it will add negligible amounts to your food. Soy bacon chips, which can be purchased in clear plastic bottles in some supermarkets, generally have better color, flavor, and texture than the bits.

Soymilk Powder: Soymilk powder is excellent for adding a little extra protein to baked goods. Do not confuse it with soy flour, which hasn't undergone the same amount of cooking that soy powder has. You can find inexpensive brands in bulk in natural foods stores or more expensive varieties that are suitable for mixing up as beverages, as well as for baking.

Soy Sauce (Shoyu, Tamari): Do not purchase cheap soy sauce that contains hydrolyzed vegetable protein and caramel coloring. Most supermarkets carry excellent, inexpensive brands of naturally fermented Chinese and Japanese soy sauce. The label should state that it contains only soybeans, salt, water, and sometimes wheat. Some manufacturers make "lite" varieties that contain less salt.

Shoyu is the Japanese name for soy sauce. Many brands of soy sauce sold by natural foods manufacturers are labeled "tamari." This is usually a misnomer, because tamari is traditionally a dark liquid by-product of the miso making process. It is delicious, but not generally available. When a recipe calls for tamari, you can use a good soy sauce.

You'll notice that I use soy sauce in many non-Oriental recipes. It has a meaty, rich flavor that adds body to many recipes. If you have a problem with yeast sensitivities in fermented foods, you can also use liquid aminos for this purpose.

Tempeh: Tempeh (pronounced tem-pay) is a fermented soybean product that originated in Indonesia. It sometimes contains other beans and grains. Tempeh has a slightly nutty taste and firm texture that many people like as a meat or poultry substitute. It is usually available frozen in 8 oz. packages (4 servings) or as a marinated "cutlet" in the refrigerator section of natural foods stores.

Tofu (Bean Curd, Soybean Curd): Tofu comes in many forms—regular (in medium-firm, firm, or extra-firm [or pressed] densities), silken (in soft, firm, or extra-firm densities), marinated, frozen, freeze-dried, and fried. The varieties most often called for in this book are reduced-fat, firm or medium-firm regular, and reduced-fat (or "lite"), firm or extra-firm silken. The regular styles are available in bulk or in vacuum-packaged plastic tubs in many supermarket produce departments and most natural foods stores. (The vacuum packs need to be refrigerated and have a "best before" date stamped on them.) Soft, firm, and extra-firm silken tofu comes in aseptic packages weighing either 10.5 oz. or 12.3 oz. and does not need refrigerating until opening. The packs can be stored for about a year, making them great emergency and camping food. Silken tofu has a very creamy, smooth quality with little soy taste, making it excellent for blended dairy substitutes, but it is more expensive than regular tofu.

Fresh bulk tofu, or any packaged tofu that has been opened, must be kept covered with water in the refrigerator. The water must be changed daily. It will last 1 or 2 weeks this way. After that, it's best to freeze it in plastic bags; tub tofu can be frozen right in the package.

Frozen tofu becomes spongy and firm. Sliced or crumbled, it soaks up marinades easily and has a pleasant, chewy, meat-like texture. Freeze regular medium-firm, firm, or extra-firm tofu for at least 48 hours. Thaw at room temperature for several hours, or thaw it quickly by immersing in boiling water, changing the water several times until it is thawed through. If the tofu is to be crumbled, squeeze the water out with your hands. Wrap slices of defrosted frozen tofu in layers of clean kitchen toweling, and weight down with a heavy plate for about half an hour.

Yeast Extract: This dark, salty paste with a "beefy" flavor is popular as a spread in England and Australia, but more often used as a broth base in North America. Since it is made from nutritional yeast, it is rich in nutrients. I find the flavor very strong and only use it sparingly in stews and other dishes that need a beefy flavor—I usually mix it with soy sauce. You can find it in the soup or spice section of some supermarkets, natural foods, or specialty foods stores under various brand names, such as Marmite, Vegemite, Vegex, Sovex, and Savorex.

Mail Order Sources

Dean and DeLuca Retail and Mail Order Dept..
560 Broadway
New York, NY 10012
(212) 431-1691
beans, Mediterranean foods, specialty foods, equipment, book

Walnut Acres Organic Farms
Penns Creek, PA 17862
(800) 433-3993
natural foods, extensive selection

Bickford Flavors
19007 St. Clair Ave.
Cleveland, OH 44117
(800) 282-8322
top quality, non-alcoholic fruit, nut, "butter," and other flavorings

The Mail Order Catalog
P. O. Box 180
Summertown, TN 38483
(800) 695-2241
textured vegetable protein (regular chunks and granules, organic, flavored). gluten and gluten mixes, nutritional yeast, other food products, soy products such as soymilk powder, large selection of vegetarian cookbooks

Lumen Foods
409 Scott St.
Lake Charles, LA 70601
(800) 256-2253
Heartline Meatless Meats: Beef Fillet, Ground Beef, Canadian Bacon, Chicken Fillet, Jerky

Arrowhead Mills, Inc.
P.O. Box 2059
Hereford, TX 79045
(806) 364-0730
grains, beans, flours, cereals, instant seitan

Allergy Resource
195 Huntington Beach Dr.
Colorado Springs, CO 80921
(719) 488-3630
unusual flours, pastas, etc.

ABC Vegetarian Foods
(a division of ABC Christian Stores)
(800) 765-6955
Seventh-Day Adventist source of meat analogs (many are only available in Canada through this source), kosher gelatin, and other vegetarian foods, plus vegan cookbooks that feature soy-free, oil-free, sugar-free recipes

Choices Market ("Natural Foods for Less")
2627 W. 16th Ave.
Vancouver, BC V6K 3C2
(604) 736-0009, (604) 736-0011 - fax
No catalog, but will take phone or fax orders and ship COD anywhere in Canada. Prepaid and credit cards accepted. Natural foods, soyfoods, allergy products, ethnic foods, spices, organic foods, vegan products. Discounts on volume buying. Friendly service.

Mail ordering yeast extracts

Marmite and Vegemite can be mail ordered from

G. B. Ratto & Co.
821 Washington St.
Oakland, CA 94607
(800) 325-3438
They also carry grains, beans, flours, international condiments, vinegar, etc.

Cardullo's Gourmet Shop
6 Brattle St.
Cambridge, MA 02138

About the Author

Bryanna Clark Grogan has been a food writer for over 20 years. Her interest in cooking began before she can even remember, and having her first child sparked a lifelong interest in nutrition. She has four children, two stepsons, two foster sons, numerous grandchildren, and a large extended family (a "small" family get-together might number 18-20!).

Bryanna contributes frequently to *Vegetarian Times* magazine, is working on several books, and is a part-time librarian. She lives with husband Brian (her faithful recipe tester) and several children on idyllic Denman Island, off the east coast of Vancouver Island in British Columbia.